THE BIBLE ACCORDING TO CHRISTIAN NATIONALISTS

Exploiting Scripture for
Political Power

Brian Kaylor
Coauthor of *Baptizing America*

Copyright ©2025

All rights reserved. For permission to reuse content, please contact Copyright Clearance Center, 222 Rosewood Drive, Danvers, MA 01923, (978) 750-8400, www.copyright.com.

Scriptures are from the *New Revised Standard Version*, Updated Edition, unless otherwise noted.

Print: 9780827203501

EPUB: 9780827203518

EPDF: 9780827203525

ChalicePress.com

Contents

Chapter 1: Gerrymandering the Bible — 1

Chapter 2: The Bible as a Prop — 13

Chapter 3: The Bible as Numerology — 25

Chapter 4: The Bible as Selectively Literal — 41

Chapter 5: The Bible as Triumphal — 55

Chapter 6: The Bible as Pro-America — 71

Chapter 7: The Bible as Warfare — 87

Chapter 8: The Bible as Rewritable — 103

Chapter 9: A Non-Christian Nationalist Bible — 117

Acknowledgements — 129

About the Author — 131

Scripture Index — 133

Topical Index — 135

CHAPTER 1

Gerrymandering the Bible

"My Bible says, 'Fear not.' We need to stand."

In some contexts, such a declaration by a Baptist pastor wouldn't spark surprise. The Bible does indeed say, "Fear not." In fact, the phrase occurs sixty-three times in the King James Version. However, as I stood inside the Missouri State Capitol during a rally for the gerrymandering of congressional districts, I found myself questioning the mini-sermon as the pastor and state representative backed a push to redraw the lines in a way that would take one more seat away from the other party.

I checked the various biblical passages with the phrase "fear not." Republican state Rep. Brian Seitz didn't say which one he meant, but none of them seemed even close to the topic of congressional redistricting. There's God telling Abram to "fear not" before establishing a covenant with him. There are a few occasions when pregnant women are told that (though in two cases they died despite the midwives' attempts to dispel fear). There are multiple declarations to and from Moses and Joshua ahead of wars. There's Jael saying that to reassure Sisera before she drove a tent peg through his head (apparently, he should've feared after all). There's a psalm where the phrase appears as a criticism of those who "fear not God." Perhaps most famously, there are multiple characters in the nativity stories who hear the phrase from an angel (since seeing an angel suddenly appear was actually quite frightening—and if you don't understand why, check out the images when you google "biblically accurate angels").

As I stood inside the Capitol listening to the rally, the remark by the pastor-politician wasn't an outlier. Organizers of the February 2022 event had billed it as a prayer rally. Yes, a prayer rally for gerrymandering. As a writer who pays attention to the intersection of religion and politics, I've attended a number of unusual prayer gatherings and worship rallies at government buildings and elsewhere (#OccupationalHazard). So I drove over to the Capitol to see how this topic could possibly be a sacred cause. This wasn't a fringe event. Several state lawmakers spoke, as did the Missouri secretary of state (who oversees elections).

At the time, Missouri sent six Republicans and two Democrats to the House of Representatives. Following the 2020 census, state lawmakers started the constitutionally required process of adjusting the lines to make sure the eight districts in the state had roughly the same number of people living in them. While Republican leaders in the state legislature wanted to keep the basic 6–2 map, some more conservative lawmakers sought a 7–1 split. Republicans wanting to keep a 6–2 scenario warned that 7–1 could be tossed as unconstitutional, thus creating the risk that judges might instead draw a 5–3 map. After all, Donald Trump beat Joe Biden in 2020 by 57 percent to 41 percent, which is closest to a 5–3 split. Missouri's districts were already gerrymandered, but Seitz and others decided it was a biblical quest to gerrymander them even more. Ironically, to create a 7–1 map, they needed to target the seat of Democratic U.S. Rep. Emanuel Cleaver, a United Methodist minister. All in the name of God.

"This is 'such a time as this.' I believe God called us here to serve with your blessing," Republican state Rep. Sarah Walsh declared during the prayer rally. Her comment borrowed a popular line from the Book of Esther, where Mordecai told Queen Esther she needed to confront the king to prevent an effort to kill all of the Jews in the land. As Mordecai urged her to save her people, he said it was possible she might have been put in that place "for such a time as this." While Mordecai hedged on whether Esther was in that position for that time, Walsh declared definitely that they were in that place for that time. She believed God wanted them to win this gerrymandering fight—even though God is never actually mentioned in the Book of Esther (nor is gerrymandering). Undeterred, Walsh argued a 7-1 map would pass "by the grace of God and the overwhelming support of Trump-supporting Missouri." This would, she added, help them win the fight against "radical, America-hating, God-hating socialists in Washington, D.C.," who "want to make government our god." Spoiler alert: the 7-1 map failed, which is why America is a godless, socialist nation now.

Walsh also praised the event organizers for starting the political rally with prayer "just like we start session in prayer every day." Looking at the crowd of one hundred or so conservative activists (and me) standing in a Capitol hallway, she added, "God can do great things even with small numbers. He did that all throughout the Bible."

That opening prayer Walsh praised came from the activist emceeing the event. Jodi Widhalm, who runs her own nonprofit ministry that focuses on conservative advocacy in the Capitol, joined the lawmakers in casting the redistricting effort as a divine mission. She declared about the state Capitol building: "We're going to claim this territory back for the Lord." In her prayer, she thanked God for giving "our founding fathers the wisdom and the direction to create this system for us." She said while talking to God that this push for a 7–1 map "is all in an effort for you, that we would live in a godly nation that glorifies you, that we can raise you up so that people ultimately would be saved." She added in her prayer:

> Holy Spirit, just fill us with a new anointing and a new passion and a new energy that the words we speak in these [Senate] offices would be your words and not ours, that they would carry a divine power. … We know that with you all things are possible. All things are possible. We know that with you Peter walked on water. We know that with you Esther saved her people. We know that because of you lions' mouths can be shut, that we can walk through fire and survive and thrive even in the midst of what seems to be great turning away. So, Father, we just pray that you would come into this building today.

While I missed the hermeneutical tie between Peter walking on water and gerrymandering, that wasn't even her most egregious comment. Widhalm started the event by reading Psalm 7:1. Get it? 7:1, 7–1. The seventh chapter and first verse for a map with seven Republicans and one Democrat. In the verse she read, David claimed God would save him from his pursuers (who may or may not have wanted to redistrict Jerusalem). That's it. Nothing actually related to the topic, just claiming God would save them in their political mission because the chapter and verse numbers align with their gerrymandered map's digits. This kind of textual gerrymandering is dangerous because one could easily respond to the proposed map with Judges 7:1, where "the Israelites were unfaithful in regard to the devoted things" and "so the Lord's anger burned against Israel." See, as the Bible *clearly* says, a 7–1 map makes God angry. Similarly, we could stick with the Book of Psalms to read 6:2 or 5:3 to push for those maps. Such an approach to the Bible makes it malleable enough to justify anything. Even a partisan redistricting map.

In the middle of the event, the group took a half-hour pause for attendees to walk around the Senate office area in the Capitol. Some prayed as they strolled the hallways; others stepped into offices to evangelize for the 7–1 map. Hours later, as the Senate session started, some from the group loudly prayed outside the chamber. But God did not answer their plea, and the less gerrymandered map eventually won out. Apparently, it wasn't "such a time as this" after all.

Bible-Haunted Politics

Novelist Flannery O'Connor once observed, "I think it is safe to say that while the South is hardly Christ-centered, it is most certainly Christ-haunted."[1] She argued such culture impacted the literary style of her and other Southern writers since "ghosts can be very fierce and instructive." Perhaps the same could be said of the Bible in the U.S. today. References to the "Good Book" regularly appear in movies,

---

[1] Flannery O'Connor, "Some Aspects of the Grotesque in Southern Fiction," 1960, https://www.thinkingtogether.org/rcream/archive/Old/S2005/127/OConnor%20Grotesque.pdf.

sports, and political speeches. At the same time, church attendance continues to drop, as does the biblical literacy of even those who do show up in the pews. It's the bestselling book, yet hardly read. People claim to have a high regard for the Bible, but most score poorly when quizzed on its contents. For instance, the Pew Research Center asked Americans some basic questions about the Bible and Christianity (as well as about other religions). The multiple-choice questions included things like "Which Bible figure is most closely associated with leading the Exodus from Egypt?" (with choices of Moses, Daniel, Elijah, and Joseph) and "Who delivered the Sermon on the Mount?" (with choices of Jesus, Peter, Paul, and John).[2] Of the 14 questions about the Bible and Christianity, U.S. Christians only answered an average of 8.2 correctly—which is a failing grade. Atheists, on the other hand, scored an average of 8.6, outperforming those who claim to actually believe what the Bible teaches. We say we follow the Bible, but too often we don't even know what's in it. The text, then, becomes a Rorschach test. We make it in our own image, finding it a useful weapon to wield without being inconvenienced by what's actually there. We have a Bible-haunted politics.

In that gap between professed biblical reverence and actual biblical illiteracy, we've seen the rise of a particularly dangerous version of Christian Nationalism. This ideology fuses—and confuses—American and Christian identities to the point that to be considered a good American one must be a "good" Christian (and to be considered a faithful Christian one must be pro-America). Sociologists Andrew Whitehead and Samuel Perry, two of the most authoritative voices on Christian Nationalism in the U.S., define it as "a cultural framework—a collection of myths, traditions, symbols, narratives, and value systems—that idealizes and advocates a fusion of Christianity with American civic life."[3] Such conflating of national and religious

---

[2] "What Americans Known About Religion," Pew Research Center, July 23, 2019, https://www.pewresearch.org/religion/2019/07/23/what-americans-know-about-religion.

[3] Andrew Whitehead and Samuel Perry, *Taking America Back for God: Christian Nationalism in the United States*, (New York: Oxford University Press, 2022), 10.

identities inspires a push to inherently provide White Christians with a privileged place in American society. As the "Christians Against Christian Nationalism" movement spearheaded by the Baptist Joint Committee for Religious Liberty puts it: "Christian Nationalism seeks to merge Christian and American identities, distorting both the Christian faith and America's constitutional democracy. ... It often overlaps with and provides cover for White supremacy and racial subjugation."[4] Christian Nationalism tries to accomplish this by narrowly defining who counts as Christian and retelling the story of America in ways that promote a particular hierarchy. Christian Nationalism seeks a social order where Christians control the levers of power and others assume subservient roles within this so-called "Christian nation."[5]

It's important to recognize that Christian Nationalism isn't synonymous with Christianity. I call it a heresy. Christian Nationalism distorts the gospel and leads Christians (and others) away from hearing and following the teachings of Jesus. This is why I capitalize the "N" instead of using the more common style of "Christian nationalism." It warrants the same grammatical treatment as other religions, whose names we capitalize (like Buddhism, Hinduism, or Islam). But it's not merely a heresy; it's a heresy done in the name of Christianity. Amanda Tyler, lead organizer of the Christians Against Christian Nationalism campaign and author of *How to End Christian Nationalism*, put it this way:

> Christian Nationalism is a gross distortion of the Christian faith that I and so many others hold dear. It employs the language, symbols, and imagery of Christianity, and it might even appear to the casual observer to be authentic Christianity. But Christian Nationalism merely uses the veneer of Christianity to advance its own aims. It points not

---

[4] "Christians Against Christian Nationalism Statement," Christians Against Christian Nationalism, https://www.christiansagainstchristiannationalism.org/statement.

[5] For more on unpacking Christian Nationalism, see also: Philip Gorski and Samuel Perry, *The Flag & The Cross: White Christian Nationalism and the Threat to American Democracy* (New York: Oxford University Press, 2022) and Brian Kaylor and Beau Underwood, *Baptizing America: How Mainline Protestants Helped Create Christian Nationalism* (Chalice Press, 2024).

to Jesus of Nazareth but to the nation, as conceived of by a dangerous political ideology, as the object of allegiance.[6]

As Tyler and others have noted, Christian Nationalism isn't just a form of nationalism. It uses Christian texts, symbols, and language. This is more than a misguided attempt to merge Christianity with nationalism; proponents of the ideology insist that what they're advocating for is just Christianity. While a few proudly wear the label "Christian Nationalist," most advancing the ideology simply call their beliefs "Christian." That's why the term "Christian Nationalism" is helpful even as some people have suggested we use a term that doesn't include the word "Christian" in it. I refuse to call Christian Nationalism mere Christianity, but I also recognize we can't pretend it hasn't been created and advanced by Christian leaders through the use of sacred Christian symbols and often with the support of many in Christian communities.

This book zeroes in on how the Bible is (mis)used to advance Christian Nationalism. The fact that such appeals to the Bible frequently appear in Christian Nationalistic discourse shows why we can't just say it's not Christian and therefore ignore it. Christians have a responsibility not only to beware of this toxic ideology but also to push back against such heretical co-option of our faith.

While Christian Nationalism is not a new phenomenon nor an ideology only arising in the U.S., it has been an area of particular concern in the U.S. over the past several years. The insurrection at the U.S. Capitol on January 6, 2021, highlighted the dangers of Christian Nationalism and popularized use of the term, but scholars had already been studying it for years and Christians Against Christian Nationalism had publicly launched back in 2019. I was among those writing about Christian Nationalism before the insurrection (in fact, I even have a cameo in the launch video for Christians Against Christian Nationalism). But even all of this isn't something new under the sun. Looking back at U.S. history, we can identify waves of Christian

---

[6] Amanda Tyler, *How to End Christian Nationalism* (Minneapolis: Broadleaf Books, 2024), 26.

Nationalistic fervor as extra intensity around the ideology spikes among powerful politicians and influential clergy.

The last major wave hit in the post-World War II years of the late 1940s, 1950s, and early 1960s. That era of Christian Nationalism, as Beau Underwood and I documented in *Baptizing America*, was largely advanced by mainline Protestant politicians and preachers. The new wave that burst into the Capitol on January 6 had been building and rumbling for several years, but this time it's primarily led by evangelical, Pentecostal, and charismatic leaders.[7] In addition to some theological differences with mainline Christian Nationalism (as well as from Catholic Christian Nationalism found in the middle of the last century and today), today's dominant iteration comes with a more extreme, violent streak. That might be because they feel desperate due to less support for culturally and politically privileging Christianity as fewer people attend church and identify as followers of Jesus. It also seems to come from ways those evangelizing for Chrisitan Nationalism today interpret scripture—as we'll explore in later chapters.

All of this means that those of us seeking to faithfully follow Jesus in our time must understand and challenge this brand of Christian Nationalism and the misuse of the Bible by its leading evangelists. Much of the time the Bible is invoked in politics and public life today comes from those pushing an evangelical or charismatic version of Christian Nationalism, which is not only shaping adherents of the ideology but also framing how others think about scripture and Christianity. That's why we must address such co-option of our sacred texts. If we feel tempted to ignore the threat—because we don't want to seem "political" or want to avoid controversy—we'll cede the Bible over to its exploiters. May we hear the words of Gandalf in *The Fellowship of the Ring* after Frodo the Hobbit remarked how he wished the quest "need not have happened in my time." The wise

---

[7] For a good understanding of the key players and ideas behind today's charismatic Christian Nationalism, see: André Gagné, *American Evangelicals for Trump: Dominion, Spiritual Warfare, and the End Times* (New York: Routledge, 2024) and Matthew D. Taylor, *The Violent Take It by Force: The Christian Movement That Is Threatening Our Democracy* (Minneapolis: Broadleaf Books, 2024).

wizard responded: "So do all who live to see such times. But that is not for them to decide. All we have to decide is what to do with the time that is given to us."[8]

Pushing Back

Perspective matters. When my son was two, he grabbed my digital camera and ran around taking photos. Looking at his photography, I noticed he took a close-up shot of every single closed door in the house. Since he could not open the doors at that time, I guess he spent more time thinking about those barriers than I did. I also enjoyed his photos of our wall hangings. The paintings seem right to me at eye level. In his photos, however, they were way up in the sky as he stood underneath them and looked up with the camera. How we look at something matters. It impacts what we notice and what we completely miss.

While many journalists covered the legislative debate about redistricting in Missouri and a couple even reported from the prayer rally I attended, every single story ignored the use of the Bible to support gerrymandering. The prayer event became in their reports just another political rally. Additionally, no other ministers—besides those pushing for partisan redistricting—showed up with me to observe the rally. It is this unique perspective as a reporter and Baptist minister with a Ph.D. in political communication that gave rise to this book. I've served as a pastor and in various other roles at churches and denominational bodies. I've also taught communication, media, and advocacy courses at a public university and worked as a journalist for various outlets for over two decades (I started young). As a result of my education and experiences, I notice things that political reporters lacking religious literacy miss and that clergy lacking political communication training overlook. And unlike most reporters and ministers, I go to events where people deliberatively mix the two (which does sometimes make me question my life choices). Having listened on the frontline of Christian Nationalist events, I've noticed

---

[8] J.R.R. Tolkien, *The Fellowship of the Ring* (Pesaro, Italy: Edizioni Intra, 2024), 54.

ways the Bible is invoked, twisted, and misapplied—and heard the shouts of "amen" and "hallelujah" that follow such atrocious and even heretical claims.

Many people in our society and even in our pews are being discipled by these Christian Nationalistic ways of reading and interpreting the Bible. A pastor will find it difficult to push back in just a fifteen- or twenty-minute sermon once a week, especially if we do not recognize how people are being formed by other influences. Drew Strait, a New Testament professor at Anabaptist Mennonite Biblical Seminary and author of *Strange Worship: Six Steps for Challenging Christian Nationalism*, argued that we must challenge what he calls "biblical authoritarianism," or when the Bible is used to justify political propaganda, oppression, and violence. He explained:

> Put simply, any time the Bible is used to lord power over others through direct, cultural, or structural violence, it functions not as an authoritative text but as an authoritarian text. … One of the strangest realities about living in this moment is that Christian Nationalists and Christians challenging Christian Nationalism both appeal to the Bible as a sacred and authoritative text, and yet draw radically different and even opposing visions of discipleship and human belonging.[9]

As Strait noted, the Bible has often been used as part of the radicalization process, so we can't just blame Fox News, Donald Trump, or other propagandists. Perhaps Strait and I sound like fundamentalists, but too often moderate and progressive Christians have ceded the Bible to the far right, who now present their Christian Nationalist misreadings as just what "the Bible clearly says." But we are not equipped to challenge misuses of the Bible if we don't even open it. As the Pew Research Center found, 60 percent of mainline Protestants say they seldom or never read scripture, with only 27 percent saying they read scripture

---

[9] Brian Kaylor, "Notre Dame Conference Addresses 'Pressing Crisis' of Christian Nationalism," *A Public Witness*, March 25, 2025, https://publicwitness.wordandway.org/p/notre-dame-conference-addresses-pressing.

at least once a month.[10] Failing to challenge the twisting of the Bible to justify and evangelize for Christian Nationalism has empowered bad faith uses of the text.

So this book is my attempt to not only document and debunk abuses of scripture by Christian Nationalistic preachers and politicians, but also to help arm pastors, Sunday School teachers, and average Christians to stand strong against deceptively enticing ways of misreading the Bible. Thus, while I will introduce you to specific examples that you may encounter, each of the next seven chapters is also about understanding a general tactic of biblical misuse. For instance, in chapter 3, we'll look at the problem of assigning meaning to the chapter and verse numbers of Bible verses, like what the gerrymandering rally organizer did by reading Psalm 7:1 to support a congressional map for seven Republicans and one Democrat. I'll unpack the problems with some examples in that chapter, but, more importantly, I'll explain why we should oppose any such effort to derive divine, prophetic insights from the chapter and verse numbers. That way you'll be ready in advance for the next time someone tries that kind of biblical "interpretation" even if it's not an example I've analyzed in this book.

Christian Nationalism distorts scripture, twisting and molding and gerrymandering the sacred texts to fit a preferred political ideology. To some degree, we all carve up scripture, focusing on what we prefer and ignoring those parts we find inconvenient, outdated, or just weird. Thomas Jefferson even famously cut up the New Testament to remove all of the miracles of Jesus since he thought Jesus was a wise teacher but doubted the supernatural parts. Jefferson, however, kept his project a secret. The gerrymandering of scripture today by those pushing Christian Nationalism is a public project attempting to redefine the Bible for everyone. Old Testament scholar Walter Brueggemann warned about gerrymandering the biblical texts, something he complained that conservative and liberal congregations

---

[10] "Religious Landscape Study, Pew Research Center, 2023-2024, https://www.pewresearch.org/religious-landscape-study/religious-tradition/mainline-protestant/?activeChartId=5290474c7be7f05443310a078ced69bd&dialogId=a681298f8100e6c269fd58d200a7fce.

sometimes do by skipping over verses when going through a passage during a service. He noted we engage in such "gerrymandering of the text is in order to leave out the hard parts" that don't fit with our vision of God or how people should act.[11] But, he added, "a church that often gerrymanders the text will have among its company many who are 'lukewarm' (Revelation 3:16)."

"A welcome alternative to gerrymandering the text is the good hard work of teaching," Brueggemann suggested. "We are, in the United States, in for tough days in the church. We might better prepare the church for those hard days to come by articulating the gospel in its fully generous and demanding scope."

That is the struggle this book joins. Each of the seven primary chapters will explore a different problematic approach to using scripture, including viewing it as a prop, numerology, selectively literal, triumphal, pro-America, warfare, and rewritable. The final chapter will counter with better ways of approaching the Bible. Our faith is too sacred and our witness is too important to allow Christian Nationalistic pastors and politicians to co-opt it. I will not surrender scripture, Christianity, or Jesus to them. Together, we can offer an alternative witness. But to do so effectively, we must understand the dangers of the Bible according to Christian Nationalists.

---

[11] Walter Brueggemann, "On Gerrymandered Texts," *Church Anew*, January 4, 2023, https://churchanew.org/brueggemann/on-gerrymandered-texts.

CHAPTER 2

The Bible as a Prop

On June 1, 2020, President Donald Trump waltzed across Lafayette Square in front of the White House to stand in front of St. John's Episcopal Church. Shortly before the photo op, police cleared the area by teargassing peaceful Black Lives Matter protesters—including an Episcopal minister on church property.[1] Other officials from the administration made the short walk with Trump—including Attorney General William Barr and Chairman of the Joint Chiefs of Staff Mark Miley (in military uniform). Although advisers suggested he go over to the church to pray, read a scriptural passage, or meet with clergy, he instead just stood there oddly holding the Bible (but not upside down, as is commonly claimed).

"Is that your Bible?" a reporter shouted.[2]

"It's *a* Bible," Trump responded.

Not his Bible, just a Bible. We later learned he had gotten the Bible from his daughter and adviser Ivanka, who was carrying it in her $1,540 designer bag (which goes to show that not everyone who carries a Bible actually reads it as they vainly seek to squeeze through

---

[1] Jack Jenkins, "Ahead of Trump Bible Photo Op, Police Forcibly Expel Priest From St. John's Church Near White House," *Religion News Service*, June 2, 2020, https://religionnews.com/2020/06/02/ahead-of-trump-bible-photo-op-police-forcibly-expel-priest-from-st-johns-church-near-white-house.

[2] Katie Rogers, "Protesters Dispersed with Tear Gas So Trump Could Pose at Church," *New York Times*, June 1, 2020, https://www.nytimes.com/2020/06/01/us/politics/trump-st-johns-church-bible.html.

the eye of a needle). Despite that, Trump's prominent evangelical supporters like Franklin Graham and Robert Jeffress quickly praised the moment as proof of Trump's Christian leadership and a recognition of the Bible's power for the nation. Others, however, criticized Trump's behavior. Michael Curry, then the presiding bishop of the Episcopal Church, blasted Trump for having "used a church building and the Holy Bible for partisan political purposes. This was done in a time of deep hurt and pain in our country, and his action did nothing to help us or to heal us."[3] Similarly, Jesuit priest and author James Martin attacked the whole charade for treating the Bible like a political prop:

> Using the Bible as a prop while talking about sending in the military, bragging about how your country is the greatest in the world, and publicly mocking people on a daily basis, is pretty much the opposite of all Jesus stood for. ... Let me be clear. This is revolting. The Bible is not a prop. A church is not a photo op. Religion is not a political tool. And God is not a plaything."[4]

Author Kaitlyn Schiess later offered a similar critique in her book *The Ballot and the Bible*: "For many Americans, the scene epitomized the relationship between scripture and politics: The Bible is a prop, a tool for leaders to exploit for their purposes."[5] Trump held the Bible but didn't read from it. Trump posed with the Bible but didn't consider its teachings. Trump lifted up the Bible but only to bring attention to himself. For him it wasn't a holy book but just *a* book.

Nearly four years later, Trump again made headlines for holding up a Bible. During Holy Week in 2024, the past and future president became a Bible salesman. As he appeared to both read from a script and add off-the-cuff remarks, he urged people to buy a "God Bless the USA Bible" that features an American flag on the cover and

---

[3] Dylan Stableford, "Trump Claims 'Most Religious Leaders Loved' His Church Photo Op," *Yahoo News*, June 3, 2020, https://www.yahoo.com/news/trump-religious-leaders-tear-gas-bunker-inspection-154132447.html.

[4] Stableford, "Trump Claims."

[5] Kaityln Schiess, *The Ballot and the Bible: How Scripture Has Been Used and Abused in American Politics and Where We Go from Here* (Grand Rapids, MI: Brazos Press, 2023), 1.

patriotic texts added inside like the U.S. Constitution, Declaration of Independence, Pledge of Allegiance to the U.S. Flag, and lyrics to Lee Greenwood's "God Bless the U.S.A." For just sixty dollars (and expensive shipping), one could get this version of the Bible dressed up in Christian Nationalistic garb. Ironically, this "patriotic" version was printed in China and in a translation authorized by a British monarch.

"All Americans need a Bible in their home, and I have many. It's my favorite book," Trump claimed as he held the Bible while standing in front of a row of U.S. flags. "I think you all should get a copy of God Bless the USA Bible now and help spread our Christian values with others. There you have it. Let's make America pray again."[6]

It's important to note that Trump held up this flagged Bible during his presidential campaign to return to the White House. So it wasn't just about making money but also about depicting himself as a patriotic and godly politician. In fact, he worked in campaign rhetoric as he introduced the Bible, like attacking the media and left-wing groups and claiming that "it's a very sad thing that's going on in our country, but we're going to get it turned around" by bringing back Christianity to "make America great again." Trump made at least $300,000 in 2024 for his endorsement of the God Bless the USA Bible.[7] And Greenwood's company later released "special" editions that put Trump's name on the cover, including one commemorating "the day God intervened" (when Trump survived an assassination attempt) and multiple seventy-dollar versions for Trump's 2025 inauguration. Additionally, there have been other "special" editions like a military camo cover one, a $100 "golden age" one celebrating Trump and adding the presidential seal along with the U.S. flag on a golden cover, and a $1,000 version signed by Trump (though I'd prefer one signed by Moses and Paul).

---

[6] Watch the video: Lee Greenwood, "God Bless the USA Bible," YouTube, March 26, 2024, https://www.youtube.com/watch?v=noezEB6BKno.

[7] Edward Helmore, "Trump Reveals He Made $300,000 Selling Bibles and Has Big Cryptocurrency Stash," *London Guardian*, August 16, 2024, https://www.theguardian.com/us-news/article/2024/aug/16/trump-civil-penalties-finance-disclosure.

The gross, unholy grift led many people to question the appropriateness of him hawking the Bible—especially during Holy Week, when Christians celebrate the death and resurrection of Jesus—like it's steak, vodka, trading cards, golden sneakers, or some other Trump-branded product. Late-night comics mocked the move. And former GOP Congresswoman Liz Cheney trolled Trump's advertisement by encouraging the thrice-married salesman to purchase one for himself and read Exodus 20:14, which prohibits adultery.[8] Yet, beyond the grift and the heretical move of putting a national flag on the cover and national documents inside like they're sacred texts, the whole episode demonstrated another effort by Trump to appear holy by holding up a Bible without any attempt to actually engage with its teachings. Unfortunately, he's not alone in treating the Bible as if it's just a magical object like a witch's talisman or a game show's immunity idol.

I Have Hidden Your Word

"The B-I-B-L-E, yes that's the book for me. I stand alone on the word of God, the B-I-B-L-E."

I grew up singing songs like that and hearing sermons about the importance of reading the Bible. I still believe that. But there are times when some Christians take the idea of standing on the Bible a bit too literally. Let's consider a couple of examples from the world of business to see the problem with viewing the Bible as just a magical prop.

In 2022, as a new Chick-fil-A restaurant was about to be built in Texas, the local franchise owners knew they wanted to do something to bless the new endeavor. So they turned to the Bible.

"When the first concrete was poured on the restaurant site, it was important to us that a Bible be laid into the foundation of Chick-fil-A Marshall," they wrote on the store's Facebook page.[9]

---

[8] Sarah Fortinsky, "Cheney Trolls Trump Over Bible Sale, Suggests He Read Verse on Adultery," *The Hill*, March 25, 2024, https://thehill.com/homenews/campaign/4558230-cheney-trolls-trump-over-bible-sale-suggests-he-read-verse-on-adultery.

[9] Nicole VanDyke, "Texas Chick-fil-A Owners Bury Open Bible in Building's Foundation," *Christian Post*, January 29, 2022, https://www.christianpost.com/news/texas-chick-fil-a-owners-bury-bible-in-buildings-foundation.html.

Yes, that's correct: the franchise owners had one of their children put a Bible in the hole so it could be covered in concrete. Then they built on top of that, though they didn't specify where in the restaurant you can now stand on the word of God (I just hope it's not one of the throne rooms). With their post, they even included photos of the Bible about to be desecrated, though they later took down the post and the photos after criticism. Traditionally, tossing things in a construction site before adding cement hasn't been an act of honor (just ask Jimmy Hoffa). Rather than the Bible being used for evangelism or discipleship, it's being treated like a good-luck charm or voodoo trinket. That's not taking the Bible seriously but instead using it as a prop.

Or consider the jewelry you can buy to always have the Bible with you … at least according to the advertisement. Tanaor Jewelry is a line of necklaces, bracelets, and rings that feature "all of God's word engraved" on them. But don't worry, these are not going to weigh you down. These golden yokes are light.

"At the centerpiece of the Tanaor collection is our special nanochip, onto which the entire KJV Bible is engraved—over 3.1 million letters," the shop explains on its website. "Every piece in the collection contains this unique nanochip, so you and your loved ones can keep the word of God close to your heart at all times."[10]

The idea to "keep the word of God close to your heart" wasn't meant to be taken literally in a physical sense. And since one doesn't learn the Bible by osmosis, just wearing it won't make one godlier. You have to actually read it. Oh, but don't worry, the company says you can read it if you have "a professional microscope with 10,000x magnification." Because I always carry one of those around! (For comparison, the average high school science class microscope only magnifies things by about 400 times.) Of course, in the age of cellphones, I do always technically have a Bible with me. But that version is dangerous because I can actually read it. And it doesn't help the jeweler make money. So for a few hundred dollars, you can

---

[10] See Tanaor Nano Bible Jewelry, https://tanaorjewelry.com (but please don't buy).

carry around a basically unreadable Bible like you're Rachel stealing her father's idols for good luck.[11]

Businesses aren't the only ones treating the Bible like a magical prop. This attitude also shows up in sermons from Christian Nationalistic pastors. Preacher Greg Locke likes to claim he takes the Bible literally. He also seems to have a bit of a literal interpretation of what it means that the *Barbie* movie was a *smash hit*. The fundamentalist pastor near Nashville, Tennessee, gained notoriety in recent years by defying COVID-19 public health measures and becoming a regular preacher at the MAGA worship services known as the ReAwaken America Tour. He also spoke at a January 5, 2021, event in Washington, D.C., as part of the Trumpian effort to overturn the 2020 election the next day.

In a 2023 sermon as *Barbie* played in movie theaters, Locke held up a Bible he had duct-taped and zip-tied around the end of a baseball bat (I wish I were making this up).[12] It was rolled on so tightly it almost looked like a weight that baseball players put on during practice swings before walking up to home plate. He so deformed the Bible that it was beyond recognition as a book. Over on the side of the stage sat a Barbie Dreamhouse, though he left unsaid whether he had bought it for the service or commandeered some child's toy. Like every cheesy Christian movie, you know where this is headed. (To be honest, when I found out it wasn't about horses, I lost interest anyway.)

Holding his Frankenbiblebat,[13] Locke read 2 Corinthians 10:4—in the King James, of course—about how "the weapons of our warfare" are "mighty through God to the pulling down of strongholds." He added about the verse, "It means you demolish the house that the evil spirit left when you kicked it out!" After shouting that "the stronghold comes down when you demolish it with the Bible," he

---

[11] In case the Tanaor Jewelry people are reading, that's a reference to Genesis 31.

[12] Watch the sermon segment (and see the poor duct-taped Bible): Christian Preaching, "Pastor Greg Locke Smashes Barbie's Dream House with a BIBLE WRAPPED BASEBALL BAT," YouTube, August 20, 2023, https://www.youtube.com/watch?v=lfHN6uk2BIA.

[13] I should trademark that.

violently swung the bat to repeatedly bash the Bible onto the Barbie Dreamhouse. The congregation cheered and applauded as plastic bits flew around the stage.

"You got to get in the Bible and beat that stronghold to death," he added after victoriously tossing his bat—and the Bible being held hostage—like he had just hit a home run.

Locke had started his odd sermon illustration by holding up the bat and declaring about the thing wrapped around it: "That is a Bible." And he suggested they "start selling some biblebats in the name of Jesus" in the church's store. While it was technically a Bible, it was really just a prop. He wasn't treating it like a sacred text. He wasn't treating it like a book he believed offered insights into knowing God and living a more fulfilled life. Even his metaphor didn't actually work—because it wasn't really the Bible demolishing the Barbie Dreamhouse; it was the bat. In fact, the bat could've destroyed the dollhouse more effectively without the padding wrapped around it. So technically the Bible made it less of a weapon and less mighty for tearing down an *alleged* stronghold (emphasis on alleged). Rather than a Bible destroying the stronghold, we saw a wild man using a bat to destroy a dollhouse *and* a Bible.

No Graven Images

As Moses came down the mountain with the tablets of the Ten Commandments, Joshua said he heard "the sounds of war in the camp." But Moses lamented that it was instead celebratory singing. However, in state legislatures across the country, the sounds surrounding the Ten Commandments are actually shouts for war.

Texas lawmakers in 2023 pushed a bill to require every public school classroom in the state to prominently display a King James Version of the Ten Commandments. The bill passed the Senate before dying in the House. But it still marked the start of one of the most significant efforts in decades to transform public schools into Sunday Schools (though hopefully they won't draw the adultery commandment during art class). Lawmakers in Louisiana picked up the idea in 2024 and became the first state to pass such a requirement. Then, like invasive weed, the legislation spread in 2025 to several other states as lawmakers basically copied and pasted the idea for their own states. Lawmakers in at least nineteen states introduced such bills as a project in 2025, with lawmakers in Texas and Arkansas passing the legislation.

Although the bills say they require the posting of the Ten Commandments, most of them actually just mandate an edited movie-prop version of the big ten. It started when Hollywood director Cecil DeMille decided in the 1950s to remake his 1923 hit silent film *The Ten Commandments* with a new talking version. The epic 1956 version featured Charlton Heston as Moses and the voice of God in the burning bush (a dual role some Christian Nationalist "prophets" seem to follow today). Before the movie became a regular on TV each year around Easter, it planted itself on public lands across the country with a unique marketing campaign. As historian Kevin Kruse explained in *One Nation Under God: How Corporate America Invented Christian America*, DeMille was "a consummate showman" who worked with the Fraternal Order of Eagles to install "granite monuments to the Ten Commandments across the nation as part of a promotional campaign for his blockbuster film."[14] DeMille even sent his movie stars to some of the dedications, including Heston and Pharaoh actor Yul Brynner (who didn't stay in character but instead also praised the Ten Commandments). State lawmakers, judges, and other politicians often joined these ceremonies at state capitols, county courthouses, and public parks to mix religion, politics, and showbiz. One such recreation of the movie prop sits outside the Texas Capitol, which the sponsor of the school Ten Commandments bill in 2023 noted (though without the DeMille history).

With that, a fancy movie poster became the foundation for a Supreme Court decision about religious displays on public grounds—and now the script for "educational" posters in school classrooms. What started as a marketing gimmick became a hill to die on for those

---

[14] Kevin M. Kruse, *One Nation Under God: How Corporate America Invented Christian America* (New York: Basic Books, 2015), xv, 145.

pushing Christian Nationalism. In fact, after lawmakers in Arkansas passed legislation in 2015 to erect a Ten Commandments monument on the Capitol grounds, it was modeled on the movie ad from Texas. The sponsor of that bill now leads a group, the National Association of Christian Lawmakers, to help lawmakers across the country enact legislation pushing Christian Nationalism.

Like the film itself, the Ten Commandments monuments take liberties with the text. Although the bills claim to require the posting of the Ten Commandments, the required language from the KJV actually omits most of the text (apparently, it was hard to fit the whole thing on the movie monuments). Only 37 percent of the text would be on the posters. If the Ten Commandments are so important, why cancel nearly two-thirds of what God gave Moses? Most of the missing words are explanations, like details about what the Sabbath is or that the graven images you must not make include "any likeness of any thing that is in heaven above, or that is in the earth beneath, or that is in the water under the earth."[15] And it says in the last commandment that we shouldn't covet our neighbor's "cattle" even though that's not what the text says. The KJV instead reads "nor his ox, nor his ass." Thus, the edited version either means it's now okay to covet donkeys or people just wanted to censor the text (unlike "What Child is This?" that makes teenage boys giggle every Christmas). Additionally, after declaring "I am the Lord thy God," the bill's text puts a period and cuts out the rest of the statement: "which have brought thee out of the land of Egypt, out of the house of bondage."[16] At least the posters won't actually teach freedom from slavery and run afoul of anti-DEI rules, but the loss of context might lead us to think we're the Hebrew people. Oh wait, I think that's the whole Christian Nationalistic mission.

It might seem minor, but excising most of the text undermines the arguments of the biblical literalists pushing for the posters. And the problems get worse from there. Mark Chancey, a professor of religious studies at Southern Methodist University in Texas who has

---

[15] In case state lawmakers are reading, that's the rest of Exodus 20:4.
[16] Again, for the state lawmakers, check out the last two-thirds of Exodus 20:2.

studied how public schools teach the Bible, told me that, because of the editing, "That version does not exist in anybody's Bible or in any religious tradition." And to suggest there is just one list ignores differences between faith traditions.

"There is no standard list of the Ten Commandments," Chancey explained. "Different groups number the commandments differently. What the commandments actually are thus varies between Jews, Catholics, Protestants, and Eastern Orthodox Christians."

Despite that, this is the version of the Ten Commandments now deemed in court cases and legislation as historical and infallible. Heston may have thrown down the tablets in the movie, but many today embrace his line as NRA president as they symbolically hold up the edited Decalogue: "From my cold, dead hands!" Ironically, when Louisiana passed the legislation to post the edited Ten Commandments in public schools, it meant that in a state where Catholics are the largest faith group, the law mandated an edited version of a Protestant numbering of the Ten Commandments. Christian Nationalists like to use the government to pick sides in theological debates and determine who are the "right" Christians. That's why we've seen hundreds of pastors and other faith leaders speak out against such bills.[17]

"Placing the Ten Commandments in public school classrooms is not a defense of religious liberty, as its sponsors claim; it is an assault on religious liberty," Chancey told me. "It uses the government to promote Christianity above all other viewpoints and to privilege Christians above all other groups. It sends a signal to non-Christian students and their families that they are second-class citizens."

Defenders of these bills say the mandate isn't an unconstitutional coercion of students since those of other faiths or none can just look away and not read the posters. Those same lawmakers and activists also insist that hanging up the Ten Commandments will make society better by doing things like stopping school shootings. But the Ten

---

[17] "Nearly 200 Missouri Faith Leaders Urge Lawmakers to Promote Religious Liberty, Not Ten Commandments," *A Public Witness*, March 31, 2025, https://publicwitness.wordandway.org/p/nearly-200-missouri-faith-leaders.

Commandments don't actually do anything if people just look away. The lawmakers apparently think the Ten Commandments work like holding up a crucifix in a vampire novel.

"We just suggested to put them at the entrance of the office of the school, the library, the lunchroom or gymnasium," explained Georgia state Rep. Emory Dunahoo. "We just need help. Our school systems are falling apart with young people bringing guns to school, shootings."[18]

"I believe that if you had the Ten Commandments posted in a prominent place in school, it has the possibility to prohibit some student from taking action to kill other students," Alabama state Sen. Gerald Dial similarly argued. "If this bill stops one school shooting in Alabama, just one, then it's worth the time and effort we're putting into it."[19]

In Missouri, state Sen. Jamie Burger made the same argument as he pushed his Ten Commandments bill in a Senate Education Committee hearing in March 2025. A few minutes later, I sat next to him at the witness microphone to testify against his bill. I highlighted a bunch of problems before noting that his claim about stopping school shootings was particularly "absurd" since "the Ten Commandments are not like a magical amulet or a good luck charm."[20] But he didn't see the light.

Don't take Dunahoo, Dial, and Burger's concerns about shootings too seriously. Those lawmakers also have a record of supporting more guns just about everywhere—including in schools! Rather than dealing with the root cause of why the U.S. has more shootings in schools (and

---

[18] Doug Reardon, "New Bill Would Require 10 Commandments Display in Georgia Public Schools," WTVM, February 10, 2025, https://www.wtvm.com/2025/02/11/new-bill-would-require-10-commandments-display-georgia-public-schools.

[19] Chip Brownlee, "Senator Says Ten Commandments in Public Schools Could Potentially Prevent School Shootings," *Alabama Political Reporter*, February 28, 2018, https://www.alreporter.com/2018/02/28/senator-says-ten-commandments-public-schools-potentially-prevent-school-shootings.

[20] Jeremy Fuzy, "Thou Shalt Not Covet State-Sponsored Religion," *A Public Witness*, March 26, 2025, https://publicwitness.wordandway.org/p/thou-shalt-not-covet-state-sponsored.

churches and stores and bars and concerts and pretty much any place people congregate) than other wealthy nations, they instead want to slap up some posters of the Ten Commandments and pat themselves on the back. But unless they're making the Ten Commandments displays out of Kevlar, they're not really helping. The Ten Commandments aren't like some lucky charm to hang up. If they were, then we wouldn't see school shootings also occurring at private Christian schools and at churches, yet we do. In Christian Nationalistic fashion, lawmakers like Dunahoo, Dial, and Burger would rather have performative faith than push substantive legislation. Posting graven images on school walls won't magically make our schools safer. All it will do is make some students feel like second-class citizens in their own schools because of their religious beliefs. Time to take the Moses approach and cast down some Ten Commandments tablets!

Steps Toward Not Misreading the Bible Like a Christian Nationalist

1. Avoid treating the Bible like a good-luck rabbit's foot. It won't transform our lives until we start seriously reading it.
2. Don't try to push the Ten Commandments or other faith symbols in public schools, and speak out against such efforts in your own state legislature or local school board.
3. Please, in the name of all things holy, don't entomb a Bible in concrete or tape it to a baseball bat.

CHAPTER 3

The Bible as Numerology

After a failed assassination attempt on Donald Trump in July 2024, a Bible verse took on new levels of popularity. Google searches for the verse spiked, it showed up in numerous social media posts, and preachers quoted it at the Republican National Convention the following week. Which verse? Ephesians 6:11.

"Put on the full armor of God, so you can stand against the devil and his schemes."

The sudden revivalistic fervor around the verse emerged from a "prophetic" reading of the assassination attempt. Not the act itself as much as the timing. The shot that nicked Trump's ear rang out at 6:11 p.m. that Saturday evening in Butler, Pennsylvania. Soon, people started pointing to Ephesians 6:11 to interpret Trump's survival. Get it? 6:11 p.m., 6:11 in the Letter to the Ephesians.

Right-wing commentators like Jack Posobiec and Charlie Kirk helped quickly popularize this "reading" of the events. Posobiec, a Trumpian commentator, had previously pushed White supremacist talking points and even promoted the debunked Pizzagate conspiracy theory that claimed there's a satanic pedophile ring tied to Hillary Clinton in the basement of a pizza restaurant that doesn't even have a basement (nor does the Alamo).[1] On the morning after the

---

[1] Dean Obeidallah, "New York Republicans Flirt with the Racist Right," *The Daily Beast*, August 15, 2019, https://www.thedailybeast.com/new-york-young-republicans-go-full-alt-right.

shooting, Posobiec posted on X, "The bullets were fired at 6:11 pm. Ephesians 6:11."[2] The post garnered over seven thousand retweets and more than fifty-five thousand likes. Kirk, a Christian Nationalistic activist who leads Turning Point USA (which is investing heavily into getting pastors and churches to engage in partisan politicking), quickly endorsed Posobiec's Sunday morning homily. He tweeted in response, "Armor of God,"[3] which inspired thousands of users to hit repost or like.

The idea spread, sparking countless more such posts and memes, including numerous photos of a bloody Trump with Ephesians 6:11 typed on the picture or ones where an angel clad in Roman soldier armor stands on stage with Trump to deflect the bullet. This led to a massive spike in people googling "Ephesians 6:11." The verse went from virtually never being searched for at all to its most searched moment ever.[4]

Soon, the 6:11 fan club spread from social media to bigger platforms. Three days after the assassination attempt, Trump campaign spokesperson Caroline Sunshine spoke to Fox News from the Republican National Convention hall. After claiming that "the left is godless," she joined preachers and Republican politicians in offering the growing assessment that God had miraculously saved Trump during the shooting.[5]

"President Trump survived as they said [with] divine intervention," she asserted. "The bullet pierced President Trump at 6:11 p.m. Ephesians 6:11 tells us, 'Put on the full armor of God, so you can stand against the devil and his schemes.'"

Miss Sunshine, a teenage actress-turned-Trump lackey, wasn't the only one to invoke the numerological "interpretation" that week.

---

[2] Jack Posobiec (@JackPosobiec), X, July 14, 2024, https://x.com/JackPosobiec/status/1812532328779915740.

[3] Charlie Kirk (@charliekirk11), X, July 14, 2024, https://x.com/charliekirk11/status/1812532983519399959.

[4] See image of the Google traffic spike: http://bit.ly/3CSvd4w.

[5] Watch the clip: Aaron Rupar (@atrupar), X, July 16, 2024, https://x.com/atrupar/status/1813245618690589022.

The Bible as Numerology   27

Conservative pundit Megyn Kelly also found the timing meaningfully related to the verse. She said on her Sirius XM show, "Not for nothing, but he was shot at 6:11 p.m."[6] Then, actually for nothing, she read Ephesians 6:11. Kelly looked up in amazement at the camera, as if she'd just learned some life-altering spiritual insight, and added, "I'm almost emotional reading it." Of course, Kelly had previously insisted Jesus was White,[7] so maybe we shouldn't put too much credit in her biblical interpretation skills.

Some preachers also advanced this timing connection. Trump's primary spiritual adviser, "prosperity gospel" preacher Paula White-Cain, made the argument during her remarks at the Faith & Freedom Coalition breakfast at the convention just before J.D. Vance spoke: "This past Saturday, at 6 p.m. and 11 minutes, we saw Ephesians 6:11. He had on the full armor of God, and the enemy could not stand against him. We witnessed a miracle."[8] Later that evening during the prime-time RNC session when Trump formally accepted his party's nomination, Detroit preacher Lorenzo Sewell, who had recently hosted Trump at his church for a campaign event, made the same basic argument. However, Sewell flubbed the moment by talking about the shot at 6:11 p.m., excitedly connecting the dot to Ephesians 6:11, and then reciting … check notes, unlike Sewell … Ephesians 6:10. Sadly, none of the media fact-checkers touched that one the next day (hey, CNN, call me).

The idea that the time of the shooting proved God had protected Trump continued to bounce around on social media. People even started selling shirts with the passage about the "armor of God" printed next to an image of Trump raising his fist after the shooting. Other shirts offered less literal depictions of the mashup, like one that

---

[6] Watch the program: Megyn Kelly, "Trump Assassination Attempt Fallout & Florida Docs Case Dropped, w/ Jashinsky, Aronberg, Davis, More," YouTube, July 15, 2024, https://www.youtube.com/watch?v=6__w2lSR8Og.

[7] Hadas Gold, "Megyn Kelly: Jesus and Santa Were White," *Politico*, December 12, 2023, https://www.politico.com/blogs/media/2013/12/megyn-kelly-jesus-and-santa-were-white-179491.

[8] Watch the program: Fox News, "Live: Trump VP Pick JD Vance Speaks at 'Faith and Freedom Coalition' Breakfast," YouTube, July 18, 2024, https://www.youtube.com/watch?v=2N1ek7lc2EE.

said "Put on the full armor of God" along with side-by-side images of Trump and a lion in front of an American flag. Or another with a silhouette of Trump holding up his fist in front of a large American flag behind a rising sun and cross, as if it were an American Easter. As some RNC delegates started showing support for Trump by putting large bandages on their ears to match the small MyPillow he wore after the shooting, the Trump campaign posted an image on social media of a woman whose fake ear bandage had "Ephesians 6:11" written on it.[9]

None of the preachers or pundits pushing this connection seemed to grapple with the theological implications. Their argument went that since Trump had survived the assassination attempt at 6:11 p.m. and Ephesians 6:11 talks about the "armor of God," that shows God saved Trump. But if God meant to send that sign to us, then it would also mean that God didn't merely "save" Trump at that time but also orchestrated it all to make sure Trump was shot at that very time! Additionally, the fact that Trump was hit in the ear would suggest the "helmet of salvation" has a weak spot, which isn't exactly a ringing endorsement.

Beyond blaming God for shooting Trump at that time, other problems also arise from reading the Bible like a Ouija board. No one ever explained why the corresponding verse had to be from the Letter to the Ephesians. There's nothing connecting that book to the time or place of the incident. There are dozens of books with an eleventh verse in the sixth chapter. They chose Ephesians 6:11 not merely because of the timing but because they liked the message they could use to frame the moment. Such an approach to biblical "interpretation" is so malleable as to allow someone to flip through from book to book until they find a verse to fit their preconceived beliefs. That's not God speaking in mysterious ways like Miss Cleo; that's abusing the Bible for politics. We could just as easily—and ridiculously—turn to Amos 6:11 to interpret this as a sign predicting the fall of the house of Trump: "For the LORD commands: The large house will be smashed to pieces, and the small house to rubble." The word of God for the people of God…

---

[9] Trump War Room (@TrumpWarRoom), X , July 20, 2024, https://x.com/TrumpWarRoom/status/1814812398315790713.

Yet, this way of reading the Bible with the numerological zeal of a Swiftie is sadly common in politics today. Like with the push in Missouri for more gerrymandering (as noted in chapter 1) when someone read Psalm 7:1 to show God supported them in pushing for a 7-1 map. Such numerological Bible readings might be one of the most obviously abusive—and stupid—ways of using scripture. All based on numbers that lack any inherent connection to the texts. Of course, if you read this at 6:11 p.m. tonight (or anytime on June 11), it might more effectively help you put on the armor of God to stand against misquotations of the Bible! Then again, it's always six o'clock somewhere.

Citing Chapter and Verse

Attempting to find meaning in the chapter and verse numbers of the "armor of God" verse would make no sense to Paul, to whom the Epistle to the Ephesians is commonly attributed. Nor would it make sense to any Christians over the 1,500 years that followed the penning of the biblical letter. That's because there were no chapter or verse numbers.

Starting in the fourth century, some communities experimented with dividing the biblical texts into sections to make it easier to read over the course of a year or some other period of time. But those chapter-like divisions don't match what our Bibles have today. In the thirteenth century, a couple of Catholic scholars created ways of systematically dividing the Bible into chapters. One of those, by Stephen Langton, remains widely in use today. Then a lecturer at the University of Paris, Langton later became a cardinal and got embroiled in religious and political tangles with both the pope and the king of England—and he drafted the Magna Carta. But before creating a document that would help give rise to a new empire in a land not yet even known to Europeans, Langton changed the way people read the Bible. And that's not always been good.

Biblical scholar and pastor Christopher R. Smith, who helped the International Bible Society create an edition of the Bible without chapters and verses, explained that our chapter placements "typically don't follow a book's inherent divisions."[10] To see problems with the system of chapter divisions handed down to us, we can look to the beginning—as in the very first chapter division. For some reason, Genesis 2 splits up the first creation account, appearing between the sixth day and the seventh day. A more reasonable spot would be to move it three verses later. That makes any attempt to draw numerological meaning from 2:1 in Genesis all messed up. Do we go with the poor chapter placement or what it should've been? Smith also pointed to numerous other examples, like how the discussion in Hebrews about Jesus as the high priest is oddly split between chapters 4 and 5, how the end of the narrative in Nehemiah 6 is instead attached to the genealogy of the next chapter, and how Malachi is given an unnecessary fourth chapter that slices off just six verses of an oracle that started in the previous chapter.

All of this matters because it impacts how we read the texts. By focusing our reading on chapters, we can miss how a narrative or argument continues and is connected as one longer arc. Consider, for instance, an especially egregious example as just one verse in Colossians was carved from a section of instructions for households in chapter 3 to instead stand alone to start chapter 4. Smith surmised this was done "to give prominence to the command" to enslaved persons.[11] But it creates interpretive confusion, making that verse now seem like "a moralism or rule, rather than as one of three examples that illustrate a principle: in Christ, authority relationships involve reciprocal responsibilities." Even if the chapter divisions were done well, they still do not reflect authorial intent since they didn't appear until hundreds or thousands of years after all the biblical authors died.

Two hundred years after Langton, another man in Paris further spliced up biblical texts by adding verse numbers. Although a few people had done that before, it didn't take off until the system created by printer Robert Estienne (also known as Robert Stephanus). He created his verse designations for a Greek and Latin edition in 1551

---

[10] Christopher R. Smith, *The Beauty Behind the Mask: Rediscovering the Books of the Bible* (Toronto: Clements Publishing, 2007), 17.

[11] Smith, *The Beauty Behind the Mask*, 21.

when he put the numbers in the margins. By 1555, he had moved the verse numbers into the text. When the influential Geneva Bible came out in 1560, it was the first English translation to use Estienne's verses. Thus, the verse numbers weren't added by a theological scholar or an ecclesiastical council; they were added by a printer thinking of a clever way to make his commentaries more useful and therefore more marketable. Now, pretty much all Bibles follow his markings, which his son said were made while his father was "on horseback."

"Presumably he meant that his father took the text along with him and worked on it at night during his layovers at inns along the way," biblical scholar Bart Ehrman wrote. "Some wry observers have noticed, though, that in places our verse divisions make little sense (sometimes they occur right in the middle of a sentence), and have suggested that Stephanus *literally* worked 'on horseback,' so that whenever his steed hit a pothole, it caused an inadvertent slip of the pen."[12]

Some of the verse markings truly make more sense as accidental markings during a bumpy ride. There's a refrain repeated three times in Psalm 42 and 43 (in a poem oddly split that probably should've just been one chapter). On two occasions it's one verse (Psalm 42:11 and Psalm 43:5), but the other time it's two verses (Psalm 42:5-6) as the last phrase—"and my God"—is separated. Some newer translations have actually moved the start of verse 6 to correct that error, meaning not all Bibles have the same verses in this spot (and thus messing up "prophetic" insights from the numbers). Another odd example can be found in 1 Corinthians 9. Many modern translations put a paragraph break in the middle of verse 12, suggesting it should've been two different verses. Or consider the Ten Commandments, which are spread out over seventeen verses. One verse per commandment would make more sense and might also help us agree on what the ten actually are, as Protestants, Catholics, and Jews split the text up slightly differently. If we can't even agree on where the second commandment starts, why do we think we can draw meaning from chapter and verse numbers added a few hundred years ago?

---

[12] Bart D. Ehrman, *The New Testament: A Historical Introduction to the Early Christian Writings, Fifth Edition* (Oxford: Oxford University Press, 2012), 21.

By the way, the section titles in your Bible were also added to the texts—much later even than chapter and verse numbers. While they can sometimes help with interpretation, they also further break up the narrative and can mess up the stories. For instance, most Bibles put a section title just before Luke 10:25 and call it "The Parable of the Good Samaritan." Talk about ruining the surprise twist of the tale! No one in Jesus's original audience thought the hero would be a Samaritan. Naming the parable that is as bad as if M. Night Shyamalan's *The Sixth Sense* had instead been released as *He's Dead the Whole Time*.

I Am Cyrus

When Donald Trump came down the escalator in 2015 to announce his presidential run, many established leaders of conservative Christian groups were skeptical. While most would eventually go all in for Trump, his earliest followers were often from Pentecostal and charismatic communities generally considered on the fringes—if at all part—of the evangelical movement. Today, the rug is all fringe. One such early Trumpian evangelist was Lance Wallnau.

Wallnau is an influential figure in the New Apostolic Reformation movement, having popularized the "Seven Mountain Mandate" ideology that says Christians should take dominion over seven key areas of society (including government).[13] He later spoke at a rally in Washington, D.C., as part of the effort to overturn the 2020 election. Numerous politicians have brought Wallnau on the campaign trail to help them win votes, like in 2022 when he appeared with Rep. Marjorie Taylor Greene in Georgia, Rep. Lauren Boebert in Colorado, and gubernatorial hopeful Doug Mastriano in Pennsylvania. In 2024 he partnered with Charlie Kirk and Turning Point USA to recruit churches in swing states to help elect Trump. J.D. Vance even spoke at one of Wallnau's "Courage Tour" events in Pennsylvania shortly before the 2024 election.

---

[13] Learn more about Wallnau in two excellent books on the New Apostolic Reformation: André Gagné, *American Evangelicals for Trump* (New York: Routledge, 2024) and Matthew Taylor, *The Violent Take It by Force: The Christian Movement that Is Threatening Our Democracy* (Minneapolis: Broadleaf Books, 2024).

Back in 2016, Wallnau sought to assuage the consciences of Christians struggling with the idea of voting for a thrice-married casino magnate who had had multiple affairs and appeared on the cover of *Playboy* magazine. While some like James Dobson tried to paint Trump as "a baby Christian,"[14] Wallnau instead said it was okay to vote for Trump because God raises up ungodly rulers to do God's will. To make this argument, he turned to the Bible with a creative interpretative idea apparently inspired by Count von Count: "One, two, three, count. Batty, batty, batty, batty, batty bat." Since Trump would be the forty-fifth president if he won in 2016, Wallnau turned to Isaiah 45. The first verse mentioned the ancient Persian ruler Cyrus, whom God used for good even though he wasn't part of the Hebrew people. Voila!

"There is a Cyrus anointing on Trump. He is, as my friend Kim Clement said three years ago, 'God's trumpet,'" Wallnau wrote in 2016 for *Charisma* magazine.[15] "I believe the 45th president is meant to be an Isaiah 45 Cyrus."

Wallnau's argument was, to use a technical theological term, stupid. As with the selection of the Letter to the Ephesians after the assassination attempt, Wallnau never explained why the Book of Isaiah. It's true there aren't many biblical books with that many chapters, but there are a few.—like Genesis 45, which starts by mentioning Joseph. That could make Trump a leader who saved people from a famine but then also transformed the nation into an oppressive, socialistic regime. Wallnau explained the number he used, but not the book. It's almost like he flipped to each forty-fifth chapter in the Bible to see which one he liked best for Trump.

Even if you accept his hermeneutical approach, some significant issues naturally arise with his logic (that he's never addressed). For

---

[14] Sarah Eekhoff Zylstra, "Dobson Explains Why He Called Trump a 'Baby Christian,'" *Christianity Today*, August 4, 2016, https://www.christianitytoday.com/2016/08/james-dobson-explains-why-donald-trump-baby-christian.

[15] Lance Wallnau, "Why I Believe Trump Is the Prophesied President," *Charisma*, October 5, 2016, https://web.archive.org/web/20161102080300/https:/charismanews.com/politics/opinion/60378-why-i-believe-trump-is-the-prophesied-president.

instance, if Isaiah 45 meant the forty-fifth U.S. president would be a Cyrus figure, why would that mean we must support Trump? Could Hillary Clinton not have been the Cyrus figure? Or why didn't Wallnau see that Joe Biden would win in 2020 and clearly become the Isaiah 46 president? Why does Wallnau not sing the praises of Barack Obama? As Isaiah 44:1 declares, "But now listen, Jacob, my servant, Israel, whom I have chosen." That's even better than a Cyrus anointing! By Wallnau's logic, Obama was clearly the chosen Jacob. More inconsistently, Wallnau spent the years leading up to the 2024 election pushing for Trump's return to office as the forty-seventh president. But unlike in 2016, Wallnau never turned to Isaiah. Perhaps that's because Isaiah 47 opens by mentioning a woman. Most alarmingly, does this mean that the United States will fall as a nation during the tenure of the sixty-sixth president since that's the last chapter of Isaiah? Assuming none of our future presidents die or resign in office, that means the U.S. will—depending on how many presidents are reelected—end sometime between the years 2101 and 2181.

Of course, Wallanu doesn't address any of that because he's not a serious biblical interpreter. Instead, he just picked a verse when it suited his partisan preaching and then abandoned the interpretation when it did not. That means he wasn't actually reading or applying the Bible but looking for an alleged hidden code he could use to justify his politics. Yet, this "prophetic" meme took off, getting repeated by numerous other pastors and activists. Many don't know its origin tied to Isaiah 45; they just say Trump is the new Cyrus because preachers say so—which is actually a better argument than Wallnau's Isaiah 45 approach.

It's also worth noting that Wallnau doesn't really engage with King Cyrus other than saying Cyrus was good so therefore Trump is too. However, as religion scholar Hanne Amanda Trangerud documented, "Our knowledge about King Cyrus as a person is … limited."[16] This knowledge void gave rise to "the plasticity of King Cyrus" to invoke the ancient ruler as "a political tool," as writers from Herodotus to

---

[16] Hanne Amanda Trangerud, "The American Cyrus: How an Ancient King Became a Political Tool for Voter Mobilization," *Religions* 12, no. 5 (2021), 354, https://doi.org/10.3390/rel12050354.

Niccolò Machiavelli added myths to the man to create their arguments for what an ideal leader should be like. Thus, there have been many allegedly new Cyrus figures, including Tsar Alexander II of Russia, French Emperor Napoleon Bonaparte, and U.S. Presidents George Washington, Benjamin Harrison, Woodrow Wilson, and Harry Truman. Oddly, none of the Isaiah chapters for those presidents—1, 23, 28, or 33—mention Cyrus.

Fumbling Prophecy

The Trump-is-Cyrus preaching by Wallnau seemed crazy until I heard him in Branson, Missouri.[17] Days before the 2022 midterm elections, I went to the ReAwaken America Tour event in the entertainment mecca of the Midwest. The tour, which I call RAT for short, is a traveling carnival of MAGA politics, Trumpian "prophecies," election denialism, and COVID-19 conspiracies. I'd watched several iterations online, but I decided to go experience it in person. In between the singing of worship songs I recognized from church, I heard about how vaccines are bad, Trump actually won in 2020, and 5G networks are a plot of the new world order (please don't ask me to explain that last one because I still don't get it). In the nearby exhibits, I could even buy products from speakers, like a Trump-Cyrus gold coin from Wallnau, MyPillow products from Mike Lindell, shirts and hats praising Jesus and/or cursing Biden, artwork depicting Trump as a Revolutionary-era hero, and some sort of fabric to "protect" me from 5G radiation (again, I'm not sure how it works). It was convenient to get all Christmas shopping done in one spot!

Even at a two-day gathering full of odd sermons, "healing" prayer sessions, and baptisms, Wallnau stood out for his remarks. He walked the congregation through a couple texts, quickly using a hermeneutical approach that made his interpretation of Isaiah 45 seem orthodox. Wallnau noted that on the Jewish calendar it was the year 5783, which he decided offered an important insight into why the midterm elections would be good for Republicans.

---

[17] Read more about the event: Brian Kaylor, "The ReAwaken America Worship Service in Branson," *A Public Witness*, November 8, 2022, https://public-witness.wordandway.org/p/the-reawaken-america-worship-service.

"If you go to Strong's Concordance, there's a word in Greek and a word in Hebrew next to all these different words," Wallnau said. "What word in the Concordance actually corresponds with 5783? And it means to expose that and make it naked, to reveal what has been hidden."

The congregation cheered, and many nodded their heads in agreement. To recap in case you missed his "logic," he made a prophecy about the 2022 elections based on a word used in Habakkuk that happens to be the 5,783rd word in a book listing biblical words. (Warning: don't try that exegesis in a seminary paper.)

But the clearest example that Wallnau just makes crap up—and that numerological readings are dangerous—came on the night of Super Bowl LVIII in February 2024. Ahead of the game that day between the Kansas City Chiefs and San Francisco 49ers, Wallnau went live on Facebook while riding in a car to offer his predictions. After admitting he doesn't really follow football games, he decided to try to make his own prediction not just about who would win the game but about what it would mean.[18] He said San Francisco had a reputation for being "woke" and pro-homosexuality, so one might expect him to predict they would lose as a sign from God. But MAGA leaders (and the oddsmakers) were against Kansas City that year since some conservatives thought the Travis Kelce-Taylor Swift romance was a fake government operation to sway the 2024 election for Biden (seriously, I wish I was making that up). So Wallnau apparently needed to look in a different direction for meaning. Thus, he dismissed a repeat win for Kansas City since "I don't know if there's meaning in having it happen three times." (Pro-tip: Remember that number.)

Wallnau found inspiration in the story of Brock Purdy, the San Francisco quarterback who barely got drafted in 2022 but now was in the Super Bowl. Wallnau also noted Purdy is a Christian (though, for the record, Patrick Mahomes of the Chiefs is as well). All of this would form the basis for Wallnau's theory on what the game might

---

[18] Brian Kaylor, "Fumbling Prophesy," *A Public Witness*, February 15, 2024, https://publicwitness.wordandway.org/p/fumbling-prophecy.

tell us about the 2024 presidential election, which he called "the big game in the last days." He argued:

> [Purdy] was a backbench, kind of like unknown, and suddenly gets promoted to the front, and here he is in the big game. Now you got my attention! ... I started thinking: What if there's a message here? ... I think God's taking people that are on the backbench and putting them on the frontbench, putting them in the big game, taking people from obscurity and putting them on the field. And I think he's sending us to the places where there's a great door of opportunity but a lot of adversaries. San Francisco is a place which needs mercy not judgment. ... I think God's having mercy on America.

Having decided which team would win for God to send a message, Wallnau needed to also bring in his passion for random numerology dressed up as divine insights. Like any gambler, he pondered the margin: "Now, the question is—if I'm correct—how many points will they win by?" He dismissed the idea of a three-point margin because "it's close" and it's a number he doesn't like because of a story in 2 Kings 13 in which the prophet Elisha told King Jehoash to strike the ground with some arrows. After the king only did it three times, the prophet criticized him for not doing it more. (Again, remember that number.)

"Three number's not good," he explained. "It's a lack of resolve! We can't have another lack of resolve! If Trump is getting back into office miraculously, we cannot just love-tap three times."

"Think about this: Seven would be a good spread for a point-spread. Seven mountains," Wallnau added about his Christian Nationalist theology of the seven areas of society Christians need to take over and dominate. "So I'm going to say seven, although that's a lot of strikes of the arrows. It could be four. Four years. Four years of mercy with Trump."

A mere four hours later—after Kansas City won by, ahem, three—Wallnau returned for another Facebook live video next to a fireplace. But he didn't predict that Kansas City's victory by three meant there wasn't enough resolve and so God would not have mercy on America by returning Trump to the White House. In fact, his earlier video later disappeared from his Facebook page. In the new one after the game, somehow the result still meant good news for a prophesied second coming of Trump. And suddenly three was a good number.

"Something interesting did come out of this, and I want to share it with you. One of the things that's interesting is this is the third win for the Chiefs," Wallnau said.[19]

He started explaining why the most meaningful number was, yes, three. And a key part of his "analysis" involved misreading Allegiant Stadium, which hosted the game, as Alliance Stadium:

> Here's my point: Third year they won. And they won in a stadium, Vegas. Guess what the stadium address is: 3333. Four threes. … And the quarterback won with 333 yards. Let me repeat that: This is the third win for the Chiefs, with 333 yards taken in a game, done at the address 3333 Alliance Stadium. I think maybe God is saying we need to be in alliance, and it is three streams, maybe it's the threefold cord that isn't quick to be broken, but the number three is so pregnant on this event.

As he struggled to find some sort of divine message from the game's stats, he referred to a couple things not actually about football games. The "three streams" might be a reference to three "prophetic" groups: Kansas City (International House of Prayer), Redding (Bethel Church), and Toronto (Catch the Fire). And the reference to a "threefold cord" comes from Ecclesiastes 4:12 (and thus is meaningless).

As he started repeating all the threes he spotted, he suddenly called out to others in the house to make sure he was right about the stadium's name. His wife looked it up off-camera during the live video and butchered the pronunciation. Looking at the phone, Wallnau got it right but was still confused: "Allegiant? What the heck's that?" After looking at the phone some more, he added, "It's not Alliance. But it's 3333! That I know. Three hundred thirty-three yards. Third win."

---

[19] Watch the video: Lance Wallnau, Facebook, February 11, 2024, https://www.facebook.com/watch/live/?ref=watch_permalink&v=368141629299976.

"Someone tell me, what does 'allegiant' mean? Look it up. Someone put it into Google and tell me if it's a word," he continued. "Watch it not even be a word—which case, we'll give it our own definition. It means alliance."

The stadium's name comes from Allegiant Air. But the word "allegiant" means "a faithful follower." No wonder it's not in Wallnau's dictionary. And I don't even need to find a chapter or verse number to prove he's a false prophet (though I'm thinking of flipping through to find the sixty-sixth verse of the sixth chapter of some book).

Steps Toward Not Misreading the Bible Like a Christian Nationalist

1. If someone suggests a meaning from a biblical chapter and/or verse number, reject that argument and be cautious about trusting the person preaching in such a way.

2. When someone uses the Bible to interpret events today, consider the unspoken implications of the argument to test the theological foundations for such an interpretation.

3. Remember that Lance Wallnau is a charlatan. Reject him, his teachings, and those who ally with him.

CHAPTER 4

The Bible as Selectively Literal

During my senior year of high school, my school made news across the country and even globally because of a silly fundraiser. The student council leaders got creative in raising money for the Special Olympics. For just fifty cents (or about a dollar today thanks to inflation), we could buy a ballot—and, yes, you could buy multiple votes. And what was the election? A simple question: Should Larry the Lobster live or die? We actually had a lobster in a tank at an assembly in the gym to kick off the fundraising challenge. One student came out dressed like a ninja to lead chants of "Kill, kill, kill" while another led chants of "Save, save, save." If a majority of the votes favored "saving" Larry, he would've been returned to wherever the council had purchased him (I assume Red Lobster). But if the majority of the votes were for killing him, then one lucky student would randomly be drawn to enjoy the lobster dinner. Fifty cents for a plate of lobster is quite a bargain. But a couple of my classmates were a bit steamed by the whole thing, so they contacted People for the Ethical Treatment of Animals. Now, we were partying like it's 1999 ... because it was 1999. But even in those early days of the "World Wide Web," PETA managed to create a stir by sending an action alert that flooded our school with complaints and sparked global headlines.

The day before voting was to end, the student council canceled the fundraiser and Larry was saved. Well, kind of. By that point, it was actually Larry II. Apparently the first Larry had died after the school assembly, which still seems suspicious (I'm thinking of launching a true crime podcast on it). Undeterred, the council got a second one and went on with the fundraiser until cancel culture ruined the butter-dipping fun. At the time, I remember wondering why PETA got so red about the whole thing as their shellfish behavior hurt a good cause. But I've come to also see such fundamentalism from Christians.

There's a "church" in Kansas known for its anti-LGBTQ ideology as its members (mostly just people in one family) protest at funerals or outside churches that suggest God loves everyone. They've particularly become infamous for their "God Hates [slur]" signs (I've censored *their* hate). But my favorite response is people who show up with counter-protest signs: "God Hates Shrimp." The signs draw from a different verse in Leviticus than those the Kansas "church" people like to quote:

> All creatures in the seas or streams that do not have fins and scales—whether among all the swarming things or among all the other living creatures in the water—you are to regard as unclean. And since you are to regard them as unclean, you must not eat their meat; you must regard their carcasses as unclean. Anything living in the water that does not have fins and scales is to be regarded as unclean by you.[1]

So eating shrimp is officially forbidden. Same for lobster, which should make PETA happy and suggests my high school was pretty sinful. The popularity of Long John Silver's, Captain D's, Red Lobster, and Bubba Gump Shrimp Company clearly proves how godless our nation is!

The problem doesn't end in the seafood aisle of the grocery store. Consider some of the other things condemned in Leviticus. Eating bacon—which really makes me question God's wisdom. Going to God's sanctuary within thirty-three days of giving birth to a son (or within sixty-six days of giving birth to a daughter). Reaping an entire farm field. Cutting the hair on the side of your head or trimming your beard. Getting a tattoo. Not standing up in the presence of your elders. Selling land permanently. Wearing an article of clothing made from more than one kind of material (which rules out most things in your closet and dresser).

---

[1] In case the Westboro people are reading, that's Leviticus 11:10–12.

Nearly every major Christian denomination has experienced a schism over the last couple of decades because of debates about welcoming and affirming LGBTQ individuals. Faithful Christians have been fired and blacklisted for arguing homosexuality isn't a sin. Meanwhile, virtually all the fundamentalists arguing LGBTQ-affirming Christians are not real Christians do so while wearing their cotton-polyester blend clothes, trimming their beards, and enjoying bacon and shrimp (or, even better, bacon-wrapped shrimp). Insisting on reading two verses in Leviticus as eternal absolutes that serve as foundational principles for the faith while discarding most of the book exposes the hypocrisy of fundamentalism.

The conservative evangelical and Pentecostal Christian Nationalists seeking power in our country today usually adopts such anti-LGBTQ theology. "The Bible clearly says," and "God's word never changes," they chant while quickly flipping past all the things that they've decided to clearly ignore because times have changed. As Rachel Held Evans noted in her hilarious take on experimenting with biblical literalism, *A Year of Biblical Womanhood*:

> The irony, of course, is that while advocates of biblical patriarchy accuse everyone else of biblical selectivity, they themselves do not appear to be stoning adulterers, selling their daughters into slavery, taking multiple wives, or demanding state laws be adjusted to include death sentences for rape victims ... at least not yet. Those who decry the evils of selective literalism tend to be rather clumsy at spotting it in themselves.[2]

Self-professed literalists turn out to literally not be very literal.

And it's not just about the issue of homosexuality. Christian Nationalism frequently relies on sewing together a hodgepodge of verses while ignoring those that teach different values—like the inherent dignity of all people, the universal nature of God's love, and the dangers of idolatry and imperial power. While all of us are

---

[2] Rachel Held Evans, *A Year of Biblical Womanhood: How a Liberated Woman Found Herself Sitting on Her Roof, Covering Her Head, and Calling Her Husband Master* (Nashville: Thomas Nelson, 2012), 52.

inconsistent and imperfect in our efforts to live out our faith and all of us put greater emphasis on some biblical passages over others, this approach is particularly problematic for those espousing to hold the Bible as an inerrant text that should be literally read and applied.

A 'Biblical' Foreign Policy

Speaker Mike Johnson has been clear about why he thinks U.S. foreign policy should remain a position of "unwavering strength and support" for the nation of Israel no matter what.

"We have to make certain that the entire world understands that Israel is not alone and God is going to bless the nation that blesses Israel," Johnson declared in 2024 as he alluded to Genesis 12:3, when God promised to bless those who bless Abraham's descendants and curse those who curse them. "We understand that that's our role. It's also our biblical admonition. This is something that's an article of faith for us."[3]

Johnson, who took an oath to uphold the U.S. Constitution, made his comment about the "biblical admonition" to support Israel with military aid during a meeting of Christians United for Israel, a Christian Zionist group founded by politically influential and controversial pastor John Hagee. Johnson made similar arguments throughout his tenure as speaker, which started just weeks after the deadly Hamas terrorist attack against Israel on October 7, 2023, and the start of Israel's military response in Gaza.

The speaker isn't alone in invoking scripture to guide U.S. foreign policy decisions today. Former U.S. Vice President Mike Pence, who at the start of 2024 went to Israel to sign bombs ready to be sent into Lebanon, spoke a few months later at a conservative Christian college about why the U.S. should back Israel: "I'm a Bible-believing Christian. And I've long believed in those ancient words about the people of Israel, that 'those who bless her will be blessed, those who

---

[3] Elizabeth Elkind, "Speaker Johnson Says It's U.S.'s 'Biblical Admonition' to Help Israel," Fox News, April 15, 2024, https://www.foxnews.com/politics/speaker-johnson-says-us-biblical-admonition-help-israel.

curse her will be cursed.' And the American people have cherished that principle since the founding of our nation."[4] Fox News commentator (and future secretary of defense) Pete Hegseth shouted his support for Israel's bombing of Gaza: "Open up your Bible!"[5] And as U.S. Rep. Rick Allen of Georgia in 2024 grilled Columbia University's president about campus protests, he quoted Genesis 12:3 and asked, "Do you consider that a serious issue? I mean, do you want Columbia University to be cursed by God?"[6]

Preachers have also been arguing we should use the Bible as a guide for U.S. foreign policy. For instance, in 2024 Robert Jeffress of First Baptist Church in Dallas invoked Genesis 12:3, which for him applies to the modern nation of Israel.

"We have a moral and spiritual responsibility to support Israel," argued Jeffress, a prominent MAGAchurch evangelical. "To be on the wrong side of Israel is not only to be on the wrong side of history, it's more importantly to be on the wrong side of God."[7]

None of this rhetoric is new since the Israel-Gaza war. For instance, Jentezen Franklin, a Trump-backing televangelist who leads a charismatic megachurch in Georgia, insisted in 2022 that "Christians should always support Israel" because of Genesis 12:3. He added, "I passionately believe this promise from God is as true today as it was centuries ago. And I take his promises seriously. There's no denying God's sovereignty and his hand both in history and in each of our lives.

---

[4] Watch the video: Institute for Faith and Freedom, "Confronting Antisemitism: Keynote Address with Vice President Mike Pence," YouTube, April 17, 2024, https://www.youtube.com/watch?v=FArvf4RCnus.

[5] Middle East Eye, "Trump Defense Secretary Pick Pete Hegseth Uses Bible in Support of Israel's War on Palestinians," YouTube, November 15, 2024, https://www.youtube.com/watch?v=58gIm8je-Jk.

[6] Bianca Quilantan and Mackenzie Wilkes, "5 Takeaways from the Columbia University Antisemitism Hearing," *Politico*, April 17, 2024, https://www.politico.com/news/2024/04/17/takeaways-columbia-university-antisemitism-hearing-00152915.

[7] Leah MarieAnn Klett, "Robert Jeffress: Christians Who Fail to Support Israel Are on the 'Wrong Side of God' (Part 3)," *Christian Post*, April 11, 2024, https://www.christianpost.com/news/robert-jeffress-christians-have-an-obligation-to-support-israel.html.

I dare not test God of the consequences for denying our friendship and support of Israel."[8]

Given all of these claims that we should use one Bible verse to make U.S. foreign policy decisions, I started wondering what other verses we should look to beyond Genesis 12:3. Isn't all scripture worth following? So let's check out how the U.S. should act toward various nations by looking for references to them in the Bible:

Cyprus. *"He has stretched out his hand over the sea; he has shaken the kingdoms. … 'Rise, cross over to Cyprus; even there you will have no rest'"* (Isaiah 23:11-12). With this warning that the island of Cyprus provides no safe harbor from God's destruction, the U.S. should abandon its military bases there (including military operations based on Cyprus to assist Israel's actions in Gaza). We must build bases in places where our soldiers can find rest.

Egypt. *"An oracle concerning Egypt: See, the Lord is riding on a swift cloud and comes to Egypt; the idols of Egypt will tremble at his presence, and the heart of the Egyptians will melt within them. 'I will stir up Egyptians against Egyptians—and they will fight, one against the other, neighbor against neighbor, city against city, kingdom against kingdom'"* (Isaiah 19:1-2). God clearly promises an Egyptian civil war as what the Egyptians deserve. So the CIA must do everything it can to foment such internal divides, from deceptive propaganda to political assassinations.

Greece. *"The male goat is the king of Greece, and the great horn between its eyes is the first king. As for the horn that was broken, in place of which four others arose, represent four kingdoms shall arise from his nation, but not with his power"* (Daniel 8:21–22). Once the CIA is done sparking a bloody civil war in Egypt, they will need to work in Greece to break it up into four countries. Maybe like a new Yugoslavia moment. There might be war and genocide, but this is God's will. Don't be a goat.

---

[8] Jentezen Franklin, "5 Reasons Christians Should Always Support Israel," *Jerusalem Post*, March 1, 2022, https://www.jpost.com/christianworld/article-698962.

Libya, Egypt, Ethiopia, and Saudi Arabia. *"Ethiopia, Libya, Lydia, all Arabia, and all their other allies will be destroyed in that war"* (Ezekiel 30:5, NLT). After Egypt's civil war breaks out, we must support mass genocide there in addition to Libya, Ethiopia, and Saudi Arabia, as well as perhaps some other Arabian Peninsula nations like Qatar, Oman, and Yemen (guess we're already doing that last one). It sounds bad, but don't question God.

Lebanon. *"Come with me from Lebanon, my bride, come with me from Lebanon"* (Song of Songs 4:8). New rule: On inauguration day, new presidents must divorce their spouses and marry someone from Lebanon. Sorry, Melania, but we don't want to be on the wrong side of God.

We could look for some other nations, including trying to match outdated national names to modern ones, but these items should be enough to keep U.S. leaders busy for a while.

There's one other country we should look at for biblical "insights" to direct U.S. foreign policy: Israel. Yeah, I know, Genesis 12:3 is repeatedly cited, but it turns out there are other verses in the Bible about Israel after the first book. And the passage in Genesis frequently cited by politicians and preachers doesn't actually mention Israel (true story, look it up). Consider just a few prophetic warnings of destruction:

- *"The Lord sent a word against Jacob; and it fell on Israel. … Through the wrath of the Lord of hosts the land was burned, and the people became like fuel for the fire; no one spared another."* (Isaiah 9:8,19)
- *"The word of the Lord came to me: 'Mortal, set your face against Jerusalem and preach against the sanctuaries. Prophesy against the land of Israel and say to the land of Israel, Thus says the Lord: I am coming against you, and will draw my sword out of its sheath, and will cut off from you both righteous and wicked.'"* (Ezekiel 21:1–3)
- *"Thus says the Lord: 'For three transgressions of Israel, and for four, I will not revoke the punishment. … So, I will press you*

down in your place, just as a cart presses down when it is full of sheaves.'" (Amos 2: 6,13)

I could go on. It turns out there are a lot of prophets who cursed Israel while bringing a word from God. I can almost hear Speaker Mike Johnson scolding Isaiah for not following a biblical admonition. Or Rep. Rick Allen asking Ezekiel if he wants to be cursed by God. Or Robert Jeffress telling Amos he's on the wrong side of God.

We know from the biblical story that the Israelites were destroyed by other nations—by people who saw their wealth and power increased precisely because they fought, defeated, and plundered Israel. So perhaps the story's more complicated than just quoting Genesis 12:3. Similarly, the nations I addressed with tongue firmly planted in cheek sometimes also have alternative references. For instance, it's not all bad for Egypt. Like this word: "Whom the Lord of hosts has blessed, saying, 'Blessed be Egypt my people'" (Isaiah 19:25).

Citing the Bible to justify a U.S. foreign policy position is constitutionally problematic. But the claim that the U.S. must always support Israel is also theologically bad. It's pretty poor exegesis to read a verse about Abraham and his descendants and apply it exclusively to the modern nation of Israel. The situation in the Middle East is complicated. Proof-texting a biblical passage won't help. Rather than weaponizing the Bible to defend one side no matter what, Christians must look to the larger biblical witness and be willing to criticize any side. We should speak against terrorist violence like that on October 7, 2023, by a hateful, anti-Semitic group. We should also speak against the killing of tens of thousands of civilians, including thousands of children—with bombs made in America. To claim that Genesis 12:3 justifies the wanton slaughter of children is to curse the Creator in whose image those children were made.

Spanking Proverbs

In recent years, the Oklahoma legislature has on multiple occasions transformed into a spontaneous Bible study. Or perhaps more of a Bible study cosplay demonstrating how not to read the

Bible, specifically how not to read the Book of Proverbs. Before we get to the problem, let's set the stage with a Senate debate in February 2025.

State Sen. Dave Rader, a Republican in Tulsa who is also the former longtime head football coach at the University of Tulsa, introduced a bill to ban public schools from using corporal punishment against children with disabilities. The U.S. Supreme Court ruled in 1977 that schools could use corporal punishment and left it to the states to establish rules for its use or to ban it. In 2017, Oklahoma lawmakers passed a ban on using corporal punishment on children with "significant cognitive disabilities." Federal statistics showed that 20 percent of the corporal punishment incidents at that time were against children with disabilities,[9] though only some were then protected by the 2017 legislation. That law came about after a state lawmaker learned that his deaf nephew had been "whacked" by a teacher who was upset he had not listened to her command to stop doing something—even though the deaf child had not heard the command and did not understand why he had been hit.[10] Rader has been working for years to codify an expanded ban to protect any student covered by the federal Individuals with Disabilities Education Act. Among the disabilities he wanted added to the list and thus shield children from receiving corporal punishment in schools are autism, deafness, visual impairment, and intellectual disability.

An effort for such a ban failed in the Oklahoma House in 2023 and 2024. But Rader and others kept pushing such legislation, which is an important step—although I would support a full ban to prevent schoolteachers and officials from using corporal punishment on any student. When Rader's bill came to the Senate floor in 2025, another senator got confused and thought he was in a Bible study. Republican Sen. Shane Jett, a Southern Baptist, had been one of the most outspoken critics of the legislation. So he popped up during

---

[9] Janelle Stecklein, "Oklahoma Lawmakers Shouldn't Be Defending Physically Disciplining Disabled Children at School," *Oklahoma Voice*, April 29, 2024, https://oklahomavoice.com/2024/04/29/oklahoma-lawmakers-shouldnt-be-defending-physically-disciplining-disabled-children-at-school/.

[10] Stecklein, "Oklahoma Lawmakers."

the debate to repeatedly press Sen. Rader to justify the bill in light of some Bible verses:

> How does the author of this bill ... align this legislation that unilaterally takes away parents' ability to collaborate with the school to exercise corporal punishment—and again, that is not beating! It's disingenuous to say corporal punishment is beating a child. It's certainly not hitting him in the face with a fist as my Twitter feed will light up later. How does the author of this bill align this legislation with Proverbs 22:15 that says, "Folly is bound up in the heart of a child, but the rod of discipline drives it far from him"?[11]

Rader, a Southern Baptist deacon and Sunday School teacher, wasn't going to—as Proverbs 26:4 teaches—"answer fools according to their folly." Rejecting the premise that the bill should align with Jett's interpretation of a Bible verse, Rader instead offered a little hermeneutical lesson about what that "rod of discipline" means. He noted that there in Oklahoma they could witness how "the handlers of pigs use a rod to discipline their pigs. And they tap them on either side to make sure the pig goes in there on the straight line, stay narrow if you want to, go where they're supposed to go. That's the rod we're talking about."

"Because, you know, there are going to be times when we walk through the valley of the shadow of death, and we won't have to fear evil because 'your rod and your staff comfort me,'" Rader added.

Angered by the response, Jett then compared his fellow Southern Baptist Republican to Satan before turning to another proverb:

> I recall that Satan quoted Scriptures on the temptation of Christ. We should rightly divide the word of truth. Let's take a look at Proverbs 23:13–14. How does the author align this bill that prohibits parents from using every tool that is legal and appropriate in conjunction with the public schools, how

---

[11] Watch online: "Senate Legislative Session," February 25, 2025, https://sg001-harmony.sliq.net/00282/Harmony/en/PowerBrowser/PowerBrowserV2/20250302/-1/78399.

do you line it with Proverbs 23:13–14 that says, "Do not withhold discipline from your child. If you punish them with a rod, they will not die?" That's not a tap on either side of a shoulder like a pig. "Punish them with a rod and save them from death." How does the author, Mr. President, align with this Scripture and this legislation?

Jett's reference back to Satan questioning Jesus by quoting scripture was ironic because, if we take the passage literally, it would best apply to Jett. After all, he was the one first quoting scripture as he asked questions of Rader. I'm not suggesting Jett is like Satan; I'm just noting the logical flaw in his self-righteous attack on his fellow senator.

Rader, for his part, didn't take the bait, again refusing to justify his bill according to a literalistic reading of a couple of verses from the Book of Proverbs. Instead, he encouraged his colleague to join him in meeting teachers who work with children with disabilities so Jett could see how they use other ways of guiding and disciplining those children. Unsatisfied, Jett repeated his effort to force a theological defense of this secular bill, this time quoting not just Proverbs 23:13–14 but also Proverbs 29:17. Rader simply responded, "Thank you for the question. I answered it previously." The debate then moved on to more substantive discussions about the bill, and it passed the Senate 31–16.

Jett made two significant problems with his line of questioning. First, he clearly worked from a position of Christian Nationalism. That is, he believed Oklahoma's lawmakers should govern and vote according to his interpretation of the Bible. But that's not the oath of office he or the rest of the senators took. His job was not to codify his religion but to serve all of the people of his state.

The second problem is he did not seem to understand how to read and interpret the Book of Proverbs. That's ironic, since he was literally trying to codify his interpretation of the Bible, even though it's one that serious Bible scholars reject. Jett's problem is he does not understand the genre of the Book of Proverbs. That book is not a bunch of absolute commands from God. Rather, it's a collection of wisdom sayings, of things that are generally true. Conservative Old Testament scholar Tremper Longman III explained this well in his book *How to Read Proverbs*. Longman noted that the various proverbs in the book are not always true. As an example, he pointed to Proverbs 10:1—"A wise child makes a glad father, but a foolish child is a mother's grief." While it is *generally* true that parents will delight in wise children and be distraught by foolish ones, that is not *always* true. Longman wrote:

> We can all think of many instances when we might question this assertion. Imagine an abusive, alcoholic father, or a self-absorbed mother who neglects her children. Are the lines of authority between parent and child so dominant that it does not matter what selfish, destructive impulses a parent has, the mother or the father has to be pleased no matter what? Of course not. It is clear that the father and mother are understood to be wise themselves. Their desires would be for the good of the child and for the furtherance of wisdom. This proverb is not insisting on an absolute law; it is rather putting forward a generally true principle that depends on the right time and circumstance. ... To read a proverb as if it were always true in every circumstance is to commit a serious error: We call it the error of genre misidentification. The proverb form, no matter the cultural background, presupposes the right circumstance for its proper application.[12]

Similar genre misidentification can be seen in the handling of cleanliness laws in Leviticus and household codes in the New Testament that are used today to justify patriarchal policies. Additionally, much of the Bible is written in poetic form, including the Book of Psalms, much of the prophets, and part of the Book of Revelation. Attempting to read and apply a poem literally will lead to some problematic theological interpretations and public policy pushes.

This genre mistake by Jett was amplified by picking out just a couple of verses and insisting they be interpreted literally by lawmakers who are supposed to govern their pluralistic state according to their constitutional commitments instead of their personal dogmas. He

---

[12] Tremper Longman III, *How to Read Proverbs* (Downers Grove, Ill.: InterVarsity Press, 2002), 47–48.

literally argued that Proverb 23:13–14 applies to all children. But it's not always true. There are some children who have literally died from being punished with a rod. Additionally, there are children who have been punished with a rod and still turned out to be undisciplined individuals or who died from foolish mistakes or who died from a disease or an accident. The proverbs Jett quoted are literally not always true, but he insists on reading them as if they are and demanding the State of Oklahoma codify his inaccurate interpretation. And if someone disagrees, he suggests they are like Satan or, as he argued the previous year, that they are "defying scripture."[13] Such invoking of the Book of Proverbs helped kill the bill in the House in multiple years. As Republican Rep. John Talley, an ordained minister who has pushed this legislation, explained in 2023, he thought it failed in part because "several people were a little nervous about voting for it because they thought they were voting against the Bible."[14]

So let's be clear: The Book of Proverbs does not mandate that public schools use corporal punishment against children. The Book of Proverbs does not mandate that schoolteachers use a rod to beat the backside of autistic children or those with other disabilities. To read the text so literally is to not take it seriously according to its own genre and the intentions of its own authors. Oklahoma lawmakers like Jett who quote the Book of Proverbs to justify their Christian Nationalistic politics do violence against scripture to justify doing violence against the least of these.

Steps Toward Not Misreading the Bible Like a Christian Nationalist

1. Avoid the temptation of proof-texting, where one flips through the Bible to find a verse to justify the politics or

---

[13] Brian Kaylor, "Quick Take," *A Public Witness*, May 3, 2024, https://public-witness.wordandway.org/p/word-and-way-news-may-3.

[14] Dale Denwalt, "Lawmakers 'Thought They Were Voting Against the Bible,' Author of Anti-Spanking Bill Says," *The Oklahoman*, March 16, 2023, https://www.oklahoman.com/story/news/politics/government/2023/03/16/jim-olsen-oklahoma-spare-the-rod-corporal-punishment-disabled-students/70016228007/.

opinions one already supports. Instead, read more of the Bible and allow it to challenge, convict, or even shift your beliefs.

2. Push back against the "culture war" politicians and preachers who elevate a couple of verses—sometimes problematically translated[15]—over the words of Jesus and the full biblical witness.

3. Consider the genre of a biblical text as you read it, allowing that to impact how you interpret and reflect on the passage.

---

[15] See, for instance, the film *1946: The Mistranslation That Shifted Culture*, https://www.1946themovie.com.

CHAPTER 5

The Bible as Triumphal

On Martin Luther King Jr. Day in 2016, a reality TV host stepped up to the pulpit at Liberty University in a quest to win over skeptical evangelicals to his presidential campaign. While few evangelical leaders at that point publicly backed Donald Trump, Jerry Falwell Jr. was all in. President of the school his father and namesake had founded, Falwell was an early supporter of Trump—before Falwell fell from grace in 2020 amid controversies involving allegations of inappropriate sexual behavior by him and his wife. Back in 2016, Falwell defended Trump as a godly choice for president despite a history of affairs and other behaviors that could get a student expelled from Liberty.

"God called King David a man after God's own heart even though he was an adulterer and a murderer," Falwell said as he rejected the idea that character matters. "You have to choose the leader that would make the best king or president and not necessarily someone who would be a good pastor."[1]

As he introduced Trump during the chapel service at Liberty, Falwell demonstrated the art of the kneel by comparing Trump to Martin Luther King Jr. and even Jesus. Trump then bragged about the crowd size at the event students were required to attend, cursed twice, and offered his most infamous Bible gaffe: *Two Corinthians*. As the politician attempted to win over Christian voters, he quoted

---

[1] Sarah Rodriguez, "Falwell Speaks," *Liberty Champion*, March 8, 2016, https://www.liberty.edu/champion/2016/03/falwell-speaks.

scripture. However, as he introduced it, he proved he didn't really know the Bible or hang out with people who talk about it. Instead of saying "Second Corinthians," he looked at the script and pronounced the "2 Corinthians" more literally. Students snickered at the awkwardness, presidential hopefuls Ted Cruz and Marco Rubio both highlighted the error on social media, and late-night comics enjoyed the easy joke. And while that gaffe remains well-known—even more so than when Trump mistook the communion plate at an Iowa church for an offering plate and tried to put money in it—what's generally overlooked is the silliness of the verse he went to read. Well, not the verse as much as the reason that verse was chosen.

"Two Corinthians, right, Two Corinthians 3:17, that's the whole ballgame," Trump riffed as he apparently prepared to read the verse for the first time. "'Where the Spirit of the Lord is, there is liberty.' And here there is Liberty College—Liberty University—but it is so true. You know, when you think, and that's really, is that the one, is that the one you like? I think that's the one you like because I loved it. And it's so representative of what's taking place."[2]

In the midst of the word salad, it's clear Trump read the verse simply because it has the word "liberty" in it. Then he even spelled it out to make sure people got the connection. Get it? Liberty? Liberty University? Liberty? Get it? That's the whole ballgame.

Trump later said religious-political activist Tony Perkins, head of Republican advocacy group the Family Research Council, had picked that verse for him. Trump said that to blame Perkins for writing it as "2 Corinthians" instead of "Second Corinthians." Ironically, Trump thought that excuse would take away the criticism even though U.S. Christians write it as "2" but pronounce it as "Second." As Perkins—who has since been a rabid supporter of Trump—said in response, "It shows he's not familiar with the Bible."[3] While that's true, the approach

---

[2] Watch the video: Liberty University, "Donald Trump–Liberty University Convocation," YouTube, January 18, 2016, https://www.youtube.com/watch?v=xSAyOlQuVX4.

[3] Eric Bradner, "Trump Blames Tony Perkins for '2 Corinthians,'" CNN, January 21, 2016, https://www.cnn.com/2016/01/20/politics/donald-trump-tony-perkins-sarah-palin/index.html.

of Perkins isn't great either. Using a random word association to find meaning might show familiarity with Bible verses but not necessarily with biblical interpretation.

Liberty University's name refers to America's political concept of liberty. When Falwell Sr. originally created the school in 1971, he called it Lynchburg Baptist College after the Virginia city where it is located. Due to confusion with nearby Lynchburg College, he decided in 1976 to change the name but wanted a new "L" word to keep the same abbreviation. With U.S. bicentennial celebrations occurring that year, the word "liberty" was chosen.[4] The school changed its colors to red, white, and blue and that year also commissioned a full-size replica of the Liberty Bell to put on campus. Later, the school used 2 Corinthians 3:17 to put a holy gloss on the name chosen for patriotic and linguistic reasons. But to be clear, when the biblical author wrote that letter, the reference was not to a future school founded by a segregationist on the other side of the ocean. And most newer translations today instead use the word "freedom," which completely destroys the attempt to make the connection to the school.

Trump's inarticulateness helps highlight the absurdity of such efforts to do theology like you're playing Mad Libs. Worse than mispronouncing "2" is taking a verse out of context. After all, if you take a text out of its context, you're just left with a con.[5] Yet, this approach of grabbing a keyword and applying it without any attempt to look at the original passage is a common mistake in biblical interpretation, especially by those looking for biblical support for their Christian Nationalistic politics. In particular, this is done to create triumphalist interpretations to make themselves out to be God's anointed heroes. But this approach turns the biblical characters into a caricature devoid of the context of their actual lives and religious or political circumstances. It can be seen even in how Falwell Jr. cast Trump as a new David: God used an adulterer before; therefore, this adulterer is anointed by God like that other one (don't try that line

---

[4] Philip Michael Pantana Sr., *America: A Purpose-Driven Nation* (Lynchburg, Va.: Pen Power Publishing House, 2007).

[5] Sorry, I'm a dad.

on your spouse). Such an approach plucks David out of the text to mold him into the image of Trump. This "reading" of the Bible starts with a political position and then seeks scripture to justify it, which is not applying a passage but profaning it. But it happens all the time—especially for such a time as this.

Rated E for Esther

I stood on the West lawn of the U.S. Capitol as familiar Christian worship songs started playing. Around me, a group of mostly women and children held up their hands in worship and waved pink and blue flags with the words "Don't Mess with Our Kids." After the music, the April 2024 rally kicked off with a declaration that they had been appointed for this time like the biblical Esther to "stand for America, stand for families, and stand for our children." Amid comments criticizing LGBTQ people and praying for Christians to take dominion over the seven mountains of society, the group celebrated communion there on the Capitol lawn as similar rallies were held at state capitols across the country. Three years earlier, Christian Nationalists were among those storming the Capitol. Now, a group gathered peacefully to declare the same territory as theirs, seeing themselves as fighting a spiritual battle with worship and prayer like modern Esthers.

The organizer of the rallies, self-proclaimed "apostle" Jenny Donnelly, talks a lot about Esther in videos and interviews encouraging Christians to get politically engaged in conservative causes. She's called for an "army of women" to join her "Esther Network" for access to prayers and fasting guides (for just $9.99 a month). Donnelly returned to the National Mall just a few weeks before the 2024 presidential election to partner with evangelist Lou Engle for a new rally called "A Million Women: An Esther Call to the Mall." Other speakers at the rally included "prophets" who had pushed lies about the 2020 election and participated in rallies seeking to overturn the results ahead of the Capitol insurrection, including Ché Ahn, Jonathan Cahn, and Lance Wallnau. Ironically, the event featured lots of attacks on a woman in power—Vice President Kamala Harris—as "demonic" while urging Christian women in this "Esther moment" to stand up "for such a time as this" and help elect Trump. While Trump was lifted up as the hero of the "Esther movement," Harris was cast as "Jezebel," a biblical character who, as speakers reminded the crowd, was violently killed to knock her out of power.[6]

Donnelly's group and rallies might seem a bit extreme, but such co-opting of Esther 4:14 is actually fairly standard fare in Christian Nationalistic discourse. It showed up at the gerrymandering rally in the Missouri Capitol (mentioned in chapter 1) as a state lawmaker said about the push for partisan redistricting: "This is 'such a time as this.'" Once you start listening, the use of the biblical passage story jumps out on a regular basis. Sometimes people specifically mention the biblical story of Esther. And people often do something the biblical book doesn't do by invoking God. Here are just a few examples:

- In 2021, Ty and Charlene Bollinger led an anti-vaccine conference in Tennessee. Labeled among the nation's dozen biggest superspreaders of vaccine misinformation during the COVID-19 pandemic, Charlene told NPR, "We have countless testimonies of people that are alive today because of our work, and this is straight from heaven. God has put us on this Earth 'for such a time as this.'"[7]
- As Eric Adams campaigned for New York mayor in 2021, he declared shortly before his victory, "You don't have to be a Christian to know what Esther said in 4:14. God made me 'for such a time as this.'"[8] Mayor Esther—err, Adams—continued to make this declaration in office[9] (and in other ways

---

[6] Tim Dickinson and Nikki McCann Ramirez, "'Mass Exorcism': Christian Supremacists Take Over the National Mall," *Rolling Stone*, October 18, 2024, https://www.rollingstone.com/politics/politics-features/trump-god-squad-christian-supremacists-national-mall-1235136876.

[7] Paige Pfleger, "While COVID Still Rages, Anti-Vaccine Activists Will Gather for a Big Conference," NPR, October 22, 2021, https://www.npr.org/2021/10/22/1048162253/while-covid-still-rages-anti-vaccine-activists-will-gather-for-a-big-conference.

[8] "Last Day of Campaigning in NYC Mayoral Election for Candidates Adams, Sliwa," WABC, November 1, 2021, https://abc7ny.com/nyc-mayor-eric-adams-curtis-sliwa-election/11187504.

[9] Dana Rubinstein, Grace Ashford, and Jeffery C. Mays, "Mayor Adams Clashes with Albany Democrats Over His Crime Plan," *New York Times*, Feb. 9, 2022, https://www.nytimes.com/2022/02/09/nyregion/eric-adams-albany.html.

has shown that a Democratic politician can push Christian Nationalistic ideas like attacking the principle of church-state separation and pushing prayer in public schools[10]).

- Many other would-be Esthers have lost in such a time as this. Like Mark Sherwood, a former member of the Christian bodybuilding group the Power Team (who I saw perform multiple times as a teenager). As he sought the Republican nomination in 2022 against Oklahoma Gov. Kevin Stitt, Sherwood said he ran after praying and realizing "my life was set up 'for such a time as this.'"[11] But this muscular would-be Esther lost the primary, coming in third place and more than fifty-five percentage points behind Stitt. Similarly, as former U.S. Vice President Mike Pence campaigned for Arizona gubernatorial hopeful Karrin Taylor Robson that same year, he declared, "Arizona needs Karrin Taylor Robson in the statehouse 'for such a time as this.'"[12] Robson was rejected like Vashti, so apparently the state is now doomed without its Esther.

- At a ReAwaken America Tour event in 2022, Mark Burns, a Pentecostal preacher in South Carolina and failed candidate running for U.S. Congress, told people it was time to fight Democrats and "fake Republicans" like Sen. Lindsey Graham: "We're under demonic attack. It is a divine appointment that God has appointed you 'for such a time as this.'"[13] At another RAT event that year, emcee Clay Clark brought people on stage to pray for Eric Trump and declared, "I believe that God has chosen the Trump

---

[10] Brian Kaylor, "When Prayer Isn't the Answer," *A Public Witness*, March 2, 2023, https://publicwitness.wordandway.org/p/when-prayer-isnt-the-answer.

[11] Andrea DenHoed, "GOP Gubernatorial Primary: Stitt Challengers Find Common Theme," *NonDoc*, June 27, 2022, https://nondoc.com/2022/06/27/gop-gubernatorial-primary-stitt-three-challengers.

[12] "Former VP Mike Pence Speaks at Peoria Rally for GOP Candidate Karrin Taylor Robson," CBS-5, July 22, 2022, https://www.azfamily.com/2022/07/22/former-vp-mike-pence-speaks-peoria-rally-gop-candidate-karrin-robson.

[13] Thrivetime Show, "Pastor Mark Burns / Nothing Is as Powerful as Changed Mind," Rumble, 2022, https://rumble.com/v15b0zd-pastor-mark-burns-nothing-is-as-powerful-as-changed-mind.html.

family 'for such a time as this' to fight for us."[14] During a RAT event in 2023 at Trump Doral, the head of "Pastors for Trump" prayed for Trump, who, he said, "God has anointed and appointed [him] 'for such a time as this.'"[15]

- During an October 16, 2023, campaign rally for Trump, an Assemblies of God minister opened the rally with a prayer for God's "anointing" on Trump. The pastor added, "We thank you for his leadership. And, Lord, we thank you like Esther in the Old Testament, who was brought forth 'for such a time as this,' we thank you for a man that has been brought forth 'for such a time as this' in the world. And as the world is in turmoil, make Donald J. Trump a trumpet in the earth for what you're about to do."[16] Such invoking of Trump as called "for such a time of this" actually occurred in multiple prayers at his rallies for the 2024 campaign. Similarly, South Dakota Gov. Kristi Noem declared during the 2024 Republican National Convention: "President Donald J. Trump is the leader we need 'for such a time as this.'"[17] Others at the convention also invoked the phrase to describe Trump, including his longtime spiritual advisor, Paula White-Cain, and Detroit pastor Lorenzo Sewell, who used the Ephesians 6:11 argument to say Jesus had saved Trump from being killed at 6:11 p.m. "for such a time as this" (an argument Sewell repeated at Trump's inauguration in 2025).

- As Karoline Leavitt, White House press secretary for the second Trump administration, tried to justify the Pentagon providing troops and military aircraft to detain and deport

---

[14] Thrivetime Show, "ReAwaken America Tour—Batavia—Day 1," Rumble, August 12, 2022, https://rumble.com/v1fq0yv-reawaken-america-tour-batavia-day-1.html.

[15] Brian Kaylor (@BrianKaylor), X, May 12, 2023, https://x.com/BrianKaylor/status/1657136726907707392.

[16] Brian Kaylor, "Prayers of the MAGA Faithful," *A Public Witness*, January 9, 2024, https://publicwitness.wordandway.org/p/prayers-of-the-maga-faithful.

[17] Brian Kaylor, "The Bible According to the RNC," *A Public Witness*, July 18, 2024, https://publicwitness.wordandway.org/p/the-bible-according-to-the-rnc.

immigrants, she turned to a story about saving an immigrant people from a racist regime: "The American people have been waiting 'for such a time as this' for our Department of Defense to actually implement homeland security seriously."[18] Of course, people trying to take "homeland security seriously" is basically what Esther had to oppose in the biblical story!

As these examples and many others reveal, just about *any* time can be *such a* time for almost anyone. But not all times actually fit the biblical story.

As a quick refresher on the biblical narrative, Esther became the Persian queen almost by accident and despite her Jewish identity. Her new husband, King Ahasuerus (also referred to as King Xerxes), was convinced by one of his advisors, Haman, to order a massacre of all the Jews in the empire out of their perceived disloyalty, embodied in the refusal by a man named Mordecai to bow down before Haman. Mordecai just happened to be the man who had raised Esther as his own daughter after the death of her parents. He also had spoiled a plot to assassinate the king by reporting it to her. When he got word of the planned massacre of the Jews, he implored Esther to intercede with Ahasuerus. But she hesitated, fearing the king's wrath. That prompted Mordecai to reply to Esther, "Do not think that in the king's palace you will escape any more than all the other Jews. For if you keep silence at such a time as this, relief and deliverance will rise for the Jews from another quarter, but you and your father's family will perish. Who knows? Perhaps you have come to royal dignity for just such a time as this." That speech inspired her to act. A wild turn of events wraps up the story. Mordecai was honored rather than hung. Haman was executed by the king, though not for a crime he actually committed. And while the king couldn't formally renounce his decree, the Jews were empowered to defend themselves from attack and successfully defeated the sons and followers of Haman who sought their demise.

---

[18] Lolita C. Baldor and Tara Capp, "Pentagon Is Sending 1,500 Active Duty Troops to Help Secure the US-Mexico Border," *Associated Press*, January 22, 2025, https://apnews.com/article/troops-border-deploy-active-duty-09324578d2b89db-5c44e0ba08f42df47.

Thus, Esther is the heroine whose reluctant courage but steadfast trust saved her people. Through her decisions and actions, justice was served and truth prevailed. She appears chosen for the occasion, perhaps even divinely (though God doesn't actually appear in the text). It's the type of starring role craved by most leaders on the national stage. Of course, their version of the story conveniently leaves out how Esther became queen because her predecessor, Vashti, in good feminist fashion refused to be reduced to a sexual object on the orders of a drunken king. It ignores Esther's not-quite-innocent role in Haman's demise (she didn't correct the king's misperceptions; see 7:8). And such a narrative can gloss over the gory violence that resulted (see 9:16). Additionally, Mordecai didn't confidently declare Esther was in place for such a time as this, as he instead merely mused that it's possible. Overall, it's a far more complicated story than our politicians (and sometimes even our pastors) like to tell.

Given the potential power of the story, perhaps we shouldn't be surprised by politicians invoking the text. But often the version told diverges radically from the biblical account. When Christian Nationalists in Texas added numerous references to Esther in the public school curriculum in 2024, it drew criticism from Christian and Jewish scholars for inaccurate claims about Esther's faith and for injecting conservative Christian theology.[19] More significantly, as seen in the earlier examples, the person most frequently said in political discourse to have been placed here "for such a time as this" in recent years has been Trump. His 2024 win, especially after the assassination attempt, led many preachers who support him to claim this. For instance, just after Trump's election in 2024, California megachurch pastor Greg Laurie said the win showed that "God has placed President Trump in office 'for such a time as this'" to stop the "crazy, woke agenda."[20]

---

[19] Benjamin Cohen, "Texas Schools Want to Add Queen Esther to the Curriculum. Here's Why Jews (and Many Christians are Opposed," *Forward*, November 30, 3024, https://forward.com/news/676477/texas-bluebonnet-bible-esther-board-of-education.

[20] Jon Brown, "Pastor Greg Laurie Says God Placed Trump in Power 'For Such a Time as This,'" *Christian Post*, November 13, 2024, https://www.christianpost.com/news/greg-laurie-says-god-put-trump-in-power-for-such-a-time-as-this.html.

Additionally, preachers like Paula White-Cain and politicians like former Secretary of State Mike Pompeo have specifically called Trump an Esther-like figure. But when I see such comparisons, I wonder if they've actually read the text. After all, the story involves an unstable ruler who cycles through wives and listens to a bigoted adviser (not to mention the whole running an international beauty contest thing). But they read that and their first thought was Trump is Esther? At least when Falwell Jr. compared Trump to David he accurately called him an adulterer instead of comparing him to a beautiful young woman.

Similarly, as Robert F. Kennedy Jr. was going through the confirmation process in 2025 to serve as Trump's head of the U.S. Department of Health and Human Services, Republican Sen. Roger Marshall of Kansas went overboard in offering his support for the anti-vaxxer: "Mr. Kennedy, I believe 'for such a time as this' … that you are the person to lead HHS to make America healthy again, that God has a divine purpose for you, and I look forward to your confirmation and working with you to make America healthy again."[21] Somehow, Marshall read a biblical story about a young woman who saved her people from execution by a wealthy, unstable man with a history as a sexual predator and thought Kennedy—a wealthy, unstable man with a history as a sexual predator—was Esther! That's not just poor biblical interpretation. That's equivalent to running over the text and leaving it behind as roadkill.

While not all efforts to christen one as a modern Esther are quite as laughable as the Trump and Kennedy examples, when politicians give themselves or other powerful people that title they neglect how their quest for power and participation in our political ruling structures contrasts with Esther's status as an "other" in Persian society. And although Esther struggled with the potential implications of disclosing her religious identity, those identifying with her story today quote the famous verse to signal their faith commitments as a reason to gain political support. But that quest for valor and desire to be the savior is an odd fit with how the Book of Esther unfolds. As Lisa Davison,

---

[21] Watch the video: PBS NewHour, "WATCH: Sen. Roger Marshall Questions RFK Jr. in Confirmation Hearing," YouTube, January 29, 2025, https://www.youtube.com/watch?v=KWb-uBArX_s.

professor of Hebrew Bible at Phillips Theological Seminary and author of *More Than a Womb: Childfree Women in the Hebrew Bible as Agents of the Holy*, told me:

> Esther does not declare herself to be the person "for such a time as this." This phrase is uttered by her uncle, Mordecai, who is trying to get Queen Esther to risk her life to save the Jewish people from an unprovoked attack through planned genocide. Esther is put in a difficult position of being caught between her husband, the king (political power), and her people. As a woman in a "man's world" and a member of a minority people, she works to thwart the genocidal desires of Haman within the confines of the system. Ultimately, Esther is not trying to gain power and prestige. Her motivation is to protect a minority group from being slaughtered.

Esther is an inspiring biblical figure. She used her unanticipated political power to seek justice and save lives. Her surprising rise to influence, which she hesitated to use, makes this an impressionable lesson about the capability each of us has to serve God's purposes, if only we will be humble, patient, and faithful.

Lamentably, many of our public leaders citing her story contradict it with their own actions. They consecrate themselves as they strive to gain power. Once in office, they use their newfound authority to advance their own ideological agendas. That doesn't necessarily make them bad people. But it also means they're not necessarily Esther figures putting their own lives at risk to save people from genocide. Let's not pretend that every politician is anointed by God. A victory on Election Day doesn't necessarily mean God has called a politician to be a hero of biblical proportions. It may just mean "we the people" have entrusted that person to fulfill the duties of an office for a brief time. That's a weighty enough task for such a time as this. So, perhaps like the Book of Esther, we should leave God out of it.

I Can Be Your Hero, Baby

It's not just Esther people like to compare themselves to. Reading the Bible with a triumphalist lens means generally associating yourself with the biblical hero, but in such a way as to divorce that figure from their context. Christian Nationalistic "prophets" frequently join Falwell Jr. in casting Trump as a new King David, not only painting him as a biblical hero but also desiring a strongman ruler. Yet, the version of David in their comparisons doesn't seem to move beyond a few children's story ideas about the biblical character who is far more complex (and villainous) than we often admit. Nor do the comparisons account for the religious, political, or cultural contexts of David or the biblical accounts of him. Rather, it's a pretty simplistic formula: David was a ruler and good; we like Trump and want him to be a ruler; ergo, Trump is the new David. It's akin to a child confidently declaring that their dad can beat up the others.

"My country, my nation of the United States of America, receive your victory this day because as your elections draw near, do not be afraid of the fraud because I am bringing that fraud down. That fraud is not bigger than me," Julie Green, who has a "prophetic" ministry, declared during a ReAwaken America event with Wallnau, disgraced Lt. General Michael Flynn, Eric Trump, Kash Patel, and others. As she spoke from the perspective of God, she added: "So to my children and to my body, I am telling you this day that I am bringing this victory. I am getting you your nation back. You are winning these elections. You are getting my David. My David is my son, and no one will stop him from taking his place, his rightful place of power. What has been stolen will be given back."[22]

Green wasn't actually offering an exegesis of scripture. She just used David as a meme to rally partisans up for a political victory (which didn't actually come as she was in those remarks predicting a Republican wave in the 2022 midterm elections). Already devoted to Trump and speaking alongside his family and political advisers, she assumed he must be akin to a biblical hero. And convinced God's on their side, she figured that surely they would win. Yet, so much of the Bible isn't about winning, and most of it was written by and for

---

[22] Brian Kaylor, "The ReAwaken America Worship Service in Branson," *A Public Witness*, November 8, 2022, https://publicwitness.wordandway.org/p/the-reawaken-america-worship-service.

people far from the margins of power. As Christian ethicist Miguel De La Torre wrote in his book *Reading the Bible from the Margins*:

> Many of us have been taught to read the Bible through the eyes of those in power, specifically through the eyes of White middle- and upper-class males. When the Bible is read from the social location of those whom society privileges, the risk exists that interpretations designed to protect their power and privilege are subconsciously or consciously constructed. Those who are the authority of society impose their views upon the text and confuse what they declare the Bible to say with what the text actually says.[23]

He added:

> Reading the Bible from the margins of society is not an exercise that reveals interesting perspectives on how other cultures read and interpret biblical texts. To read the Bible from the margins is to grasp God in the midst of struggle and oppression. ... Reading the Bible from the margins is as crucial for the salvation of the dominant culture as it is for the liberation of the disenfranchised.[24]

We don't just need to read the Bible more; we need to read the Bible more from the margins.

In contrast, consider how Republican House Speaker Mike Johnson, a Southern Baptist lay leader who has led lectures at churches about how the U.S. should be a "Christian nation," described himself immediately after his election as speaker in October 2023. He declared from the House podium that he had been put in that position by God and that the other members of Congress had similarly been divinely elected.[25] That argument was odd considering he led a House GOP effort to cancel Joe Biden's win in the 2020 election (apparently sleepy

---

[23] Miguel A. De La Torre, *Reading the Bible from the Margins* (Maryknoll, NY: Orbis Books, 2002), 4.

[24] De La Torre, *Reading the Bible from the Margins*, 4–5.

[25] Brian Kaylor and Jeremy Fuzy, "Christian Nationalism in the Speaker's Chair," *A Public Witness*, October 26, 2023, https://publicwitness.wordandway.org/p/christian-nationalism-in-the-speakers.

Jehovah wasn't paying attention during that election). A little over a month after his election as speaker, Johnson spoke to the National Association of Christian Lawmakers, which works to push Christian Nationalistic policies in state legislatures across the country. Johnson told them "the Lord" had called him to be "a new Moses" for this "Red Sea moment."[26] Seeing himself on a divinely appointed mission, Johnson christened himself as the new iteration of one of the greatest biblical heroes to enact what he thinks is God's will through legislation. Such a self-serving read of the Bible means that to question whether Johnson is the new Moses is to doubt God (though Democrats haven't been struck down with leprosy like Miriam yet).

Or consider the self-portrait painted by Texas Attorney General Ken Paxton, who was impeached by his fellow Republicans in the Texas House in 2023 over allegations he had accepted bribes, abused his power to target a charity and attack a whistleblower, and used his office to benefit himself, a friend, and a mistress. Through it all, the politician who frequently pushes for more Christianity in public schools and spoke at Trump's January 6 rally in D.C. enjoyed support from Christian Nationalist pastors in the state.[27] After narrowly escaping conviction in the Senate, he compared himself to the biblical patriarch Joseph who was sold into slavery by his brothers. Paxton briefly mentioned that part of the story before adding: "Didn't work out so well for [his brothers] initially because he became prime minister of Egypt and he's standing in front of his brothers. They're terrified and he says to them, 'What you meant for evil, God meant for good.'"[28] Although Paxton wore a coat of just one color, he ironically gave his remarks in front of a large photo of Richard Nixon thrusting his arms into the air with "V-for-victory" salutes as he left the White House in disgrace. But that was less problematic than Paxton's exegesis of the

---

[26] Tim Dickinson, "Mike Johnson Compares Himself to Moses at Christian Nationalistic Gala," *Rolling Stone*, December 6, 2023, https://www.rolling-stone.com/politics/politics-news/mike-johnson-moses-christian-nationalist-gala-123491856.

[27] Brian Kaylor, "The Passion of Ken Paxton," *A Public Witness*, August 31, 2023, https://publicwitness.wordandway.org/p/the-passion-of-ken-paxton.

[28] J2, "Marc LaHood for HD 121 Introduced by AG Ken Paxton," YouTube, January 23, 2024, https://www.youtube.com/watch?v=cMn-anVFwpA.

text. He flipped the biblical story to make himself the hero. Joseph was a young man wrongly sold into slavery for decades who remained righteous, refused the advances of a married woman and then, once in power, used it to save those who had mistreated him. Paxton is a powerful man who abused his position, cheated on his wife, escaped justice for his wrongdoings, and used his power to attack those who tried to hold him accountable. But that Genesis 50:20 verse is a popular one when Christian Nationalists stage a comeback. Trumpian pundit Charlie Kirk and others cited it when Trump returned to the White House as if he were a new Joseph.[29]

Not to be outdone, Trump compared himself to Jesus (who clearly trumps Moses and Joseph). During his 2024 campaign, he played a video declaring "God made Trump" and portraying him as a messianic figure "who cares for the flock, a shepherd to mankind who will never leave nor forsake them."[30] And he reposted on social media a small fraction of his supporters who compared his legal woes to the persecution and crucifixion of Jesus. U.S. Rep. Marjorie Taylor Greene of Georgia, who calls herself a "proud Christian Nationalist," was just one who gave voice to that argument. As Trump was arraigned in New York City on thirty-four felony counts for falsifying business documents to cover up his hush money payments to a porn star he had an affair with, she declared, "Jesus was arrested and murdered by the Roman government. There have been many people throughout history that have been arrested and persecuted by radical corrupt governments, and it's beginning today in New York City. And I just can't believe it's happening, but I'll always support him. He's done nothing wrong."[31] WWJD? Apparently, sleep with a porn star and falsify business documents to cover it up. When you're triumphally comparing your political candidate to Jesus, you've moved from just heresy for such a time as this to outright blasphemy.

---

[29] Charlie Kirk (@charliekirk11), X, January 8, 2025, https://x.com/charliekirk11/status/1877146301168578682.

[30] Brian Kaylor, "Prayers of the MAGA Faithful," *A Public Witness*, January 9, 2024, https://publicwitness.wordandway.org/p/prayers-of-the-maga-faithful.

[31] Thomas B. Edsall, "The Deification of Donald Trump Poses Some Interesting Questions," *New York Times*, January 17, 2204, https://www.nytimes.com/2024/01/17/opinion/trump-god-evangelicals-anointed.html.

Steps Toward Not Misreading the Bible Like a Christian Nationalist

1. Attempt to read the Bible from the margins. If you're like me, that includes thinking about what it might mean from a position with less political or economic status than yourself, and it necessitates reading more biblical perspectives from people who aren't White men from the United States.
2. Consider biblical characters and stories in their context, in ways that compare and contrast from your own. And move beyond flat interpretations of biblical figures that treat them as all good or all evil.
3. Try not to assume you are the hero of the biblical story, and be careful about preachers and politicians who center themselves or their movement as the new biblical heroes. With apologies to Carly Simon, don't be so vain that you think the verse is about you.

CHAPTER 6

The Bible as Pro-America

On the day after President Donald Trump's second inauguration, he went to a traditional inaugural worship service at the Washington National Cathedral, an Episcopal congregation in the nation's capital. It marked the first time he attended a church service with a sermon (not counting funerals) in over three years. And he didn't like it. Near the end of the sermon, Episcopal Bishop Mariann Budde of the Diocese of Washington, D.C., urged Trump to "have mercy upon the people in our country who are scared now."[1] She specifically mentioned LGBTQ children and migrant workers. Trump sat stone-faced during the plea while Vice President J.D. Vance gave a side-eye and others nearby looked uncomfortable. Asked about the service afterward as he returned to the White House, Trump criticized it: "Not too exciting, was it? I didn't think it was a good service."[2] He later took to social media to blast Budde as a "so-called bishop" and "a Radical Left hard line Trump hater" who was "nasty in tone, and not compelling or smart."[3] He added, "She and her church owe the public an apology." It should be noted that much of the service actually included Christian

---

[1] Brian Kaylor, "Brave Sermon Exposes Christian Nationalism," *A Public Witness*, January 22, 2025, https://publicwitness.wordandway.org/p/brave-sermon-exposes-christian-nationalism.

[2] Alex Gangitano, "Trump: Inauguration Prayer Service was 'Not Too Exciting,'" *The Hill*, January 21, 2025, https://thehill.com/homenews/administration/5098578-trump-inauguration-prayer-service-not-exciting.

[3] Donald J. Trump (@realDonaldTrump), Truth Social, January 21, 2025, https://truthsocial.com/@realDonaldTrump/posts/113870397327465225.

Nationalistic elements as seen in hymns, prayers, and other parts of the liturgy[4] (which isn't really a surprise since mainline Protestants like the Episcopal Church helped build Christian Nationalism[5]).

Yet, even with all that Christian Nationalism, the short plea for mercy irritated Trump and many Christian Nationalist preachers and politicians. Twenty-three GOP House members even sponsored a resolution to condemn Budde's sermon, claiming she had "used her position inappropriately, promoting political bias instead of advocating the full counsel of biblical teaching."[6] Thinking the government should get to decide if a sermon is biblical or not is classic Christian Nationalism. The resolution's cosponsors included Rep. Mike Collins of Georgia, who also posted a clip on Elon Musk's X platform of Budde preaching with the caption, "The person giving this sermon should be added to the deportation list."[7] For the record, Budde is a U.S. citizen who was born in New Jersey (which clearly makes her … Born in the U.S.A.[8]). A few days after the service, Collins posted again on X, this time sharing a prayer offered by a guest chaplain in the U.S. House of Representatives. Alluding to Budde's sermon, Collins wrote, "It was an honor to host Dr. Benny Tate from Rock Springs Church in Milner, GA as a guest chaplain in today's House Pro Forma Session. It was refreshing to hear the word of God without the added liberal activism. A balanced prayer from a solid pastor."[9] That's quite a claim, especially from someone upset at a preacher for talking about mercy, so I had to check it out. I'm against legislative prayers in general[10] and find the roles of House and Senate chaplains

---

[4] Kaylor, "Brave Sermon Exposes."

[5] Brian Kaylor and Beau Underwood, *Baptizing America: How Mainline Protestants Helped Create Christian Nationalism* (Chalice Press, 2024).

[6] Brian Kaylor, "After Viral Sermon, GOP Threatens Religious Liberty," *A Public Witness*, January 25, 2025, https://publicwitness.wordandway.org/p/after-viral-sermon-gop-threatens.

[7] Rep. Mike Collins (@RepMikeCollins), X, January 21, 2025, https://x.com/RepMikeCollins/status/1881765967338131546.

[8] Down in the shadow of the penitentiary, out by the gas fires of the refinery.

[9] Rep. Mike Collins (@RepMikeCollins), X, January 24, 2025, https://x.com/RepMikeCollins/status/1882832626765255012.

[10] Brian Kaylor, "The Democratic Sin of Congressional Chaplains," *Roll Call*, January 5, 2021, https://rollcall.com/2021/01/05/the-democratic-sin-of-congressional-chaplains.

to advance Christian Nationalism.[11] But the prayer by Tate, who had previously pushed Republican politics during Sunday church services,[12] was particularly egregious:

> Lord, as we come before you today, we thank you for your faithfulness to our nation for almost 250 years. The Scripture teaches us, "Blessed is the nation whose God is the Lord." God, I thank you for your presence, preservation, and protection throughout these many years. May we always remember that righteousness exalteth a nation, but sin is a reproach to any people. The nation that is a city upon a hill is truly salt and light to the world, making whatsoever and whosoever around them better and brighter.[13]

Tate tossed in quite a few Bible verses, which he recast as being about the United States, including Psalm 33:12, Proverbs 14:34, and Matthew 5:13–14. The first two were problematic enough as he repackaged statements about ancient Israel to instead be about the United States. But his use of Matthew 5 was downright heretical.

The context of the Sermon on the Mount was Jesus teaching his disciples (not merely the Twelve but probably a larger group of followers). In that context, he therefore clearly identified the "you" he addressed. The "you" are his disciples, which thanks to Matthew now include those of us today who follow him. So when he said "you are the salt of the earth" and "you are the light of the world," he was not speaking about any nation but about his followers. Thus, it is unbiblical to say "the nation that is 'a city upon a hill.'" That's not a thing if we actually read the text. Such rhetoric baptizes America and all who live in it while simultaneously casting doubt on the salvation of Christians who aren't American. That's Christian Nationalism at its core by fusing and confusing American and Christian identities.

Yet, if you listen carefully, you'll hear politicians and preachers frequently co-opt Jesus's "city upon a hill" language to baptize the

---

[11] Kaylor and Underwood, *Baptizing America*.
[12] Brian Kaylor, "Not-So-Peachy Race in Georgia," *A Public Witness*, April 14, 2022, https://publicwitness.wordandway.org/p/not-so-peachy-race-in-georgia.
[13] 171 Cong. Rec. H391 (January 24, 2024), https://www.congress.gov/119/crec/2025/01/24/171/15/CREC-2025-01-24.pdf.

U.S. as that godly light to the world. It was the most used Bible reference during the Republican National Convention in 2024.[14] Like by Tennessee Gov. Bill Lee, who called the Republican delegates "guardians of our shining city on a hill."[15] It showed up in prayers at Trump rallies during the 2024 campaign, such as during a Nevada rally: "I pray for our country, America, and that you will preserve this country, Lord, because this is the light on top of the hill. Lord, let it shine and continue to shine."[16] Disgraced former Army Lt. Gen. Michael Flynn, a key Trumpian ally pushing QAnon ideas and visions of a violent takeover of the nation, invoked it at a stop of the ReAwaken America Tour held at John Hagee's church in San Antonio, Texas. Flynn made clear his Christian Nationalist vision of uniting church and state: "If we are going to have one nation under God, which we must, we have to have one religion. One nation under God and one religion under God."[17] He added, "God Almighty is involved in this country because this is it. This is the last place on Earth. This is the shining 'city on the hill.'" Casting America as the messianic hope for the world, Flynn wanted to control the nation politically and religiously. This should raise questions about who gets to lead the nation's "one religion" as a Catholic politician made the argument in a Protestant church.

The verse from Matthew is also often invoked in Christian Nationalist efforts like the National Day of Prayer. The official 2024 NDP prayer included this request before listing the "seven mountains" for Christians to take over (which, as noted in chapter 3, was popularized by Lance Wallnau): "Forgive us for fearing and focusing on the darkness around us instead of being filled with faith

---

[14] Kelsey Dallas, "The Bible Verses in the Spotlight at Part Conventions," *Deseret News*, August 27, 2024, tps://www.deseret.com/faith/2024/08/27/bible-verses-used-by-politicians.

[15] Watch the video: Brian Kaylor (@BrianKaylor), X, July 16, 2024, https://x.com/BrianKaylor/status/1813341415625154568.

[16] Brian Kaylor, "Prayers of the MAGA Faithful," *A Public Witness*, January 9, 2024, https://publicwitness.wordandway.org/p/prayers-of-the-maga-faithful.

[17] Brian Kaylor and Beau Underwood, "One Nation Under Michael Flynn's God?" *A Public Witness*, November 16, 2021, https://publicwitness.wordandway.org/p/one-nation-under-michael-flynns-god.

and shining like the city on a hill you have called us to be."[18] It also shows up regularly at the National Prayer Breakfast, another prominent Christian Nationalist event.[19] Like in 2025 when President Donald Trump declared while in the Capitol:

> Just steps away from here in the hall of columns is the statue of John Winthrop, who famously proclaimed that America would stand as "a city upon a hill," "a light to all nations." With the eyes of all people upon us, today almost four hundred years after that famous sermon, we see that with the Lord's help, the city stands taller and shines brighter than ever before—or at least it soon will.[20]

Trump, in his characteristic fashion, took the statement even further than most politicians by adding a partisan tinge. He not only recast God's followers as the United States, but he suggested the witness of this "city upon a hill" was getting more triumphant because he had returned to the White House.

While Trump messed up the theology and some of the history, he did correctly point to early colonial leader John Winthrop as the key originator of this misapplication. In 1630, Winthrop joined a fleet of people leaving England to head across the Atlantic to settle in the so-called "New World." At some point either right before they left or on the voyage itself, he delivered a sermon on "A Model of Christian Charity." In it, he declared what he saw as God's plan for this "New England" they set off to help establish: "For we must consider that we shall be as a city upon a hill. The eyes of all people are upon us."[21] He wasn't quite calling the nation of the U.S.—which didn't even exist as a dream—the "city upon a hill," but he was thinking of their

---

[18] Brian Kaylor, "The National Day of Seven Mountains Prayer," *A Public Witness*, May 2, 2024, https://publicwitness.wordandway.org/p/the-national-day-of-seven-mountains.

[19] For a look at the Christian Nationalist history of the National Prayer Breakfast, see: Kaylor and Underwood, *Baptizing America*.

[20] Watch the clip: Brian Kaylor (@BrianKaylor), X, February 5, 2025, https://x.com/BrianKaylor/status/1887493319623581947.

[21] John Winthrop, "A Modell of Christian Charity (1630)" Hanover Historical Texts Collection, https://history.hanover.edu/texts/winthmod.html.

new colony in such terms. Although this co-opting of scripture by Winthrop is widely echoed today by American politicians and even some preachers, other parts of his speech remain less famous. Like when he used the Bible to justify genocide. Invoking the story of King Saul being ordered by God to kill all of the Amalekites, Winthrop insisted that "when God gives a special commission, he looks to have it strictly observed in every article." Winthrop added that he and the other Puritans had "entered into Covenant with [God] of favor and blessing," but it would depend on whether they would follow God's command or violate it like Saul did when he failed to kill all of the Amalekites. With that, Winthrop laid the theological foundation for killing the Native Americans as the new Amalekites just as he christened the Puritans as the new Israelites off to establish the new "city upon a hill."

Historian John Corrigan warned about the "rhetoric of extermination" that came from the use of the Amalek story in *The First Prejudice: Religious Tolerance and Intolerance in Early America*:

> In America, thinking about Amalek in the 18th century also was refined through the coalescence of an ideology of America as a "redeemer nation" called to defeat evil wherever it threatened Christianity. … And the transition from colonial status to new nation lent a particularly urgent and pointed tone to the Amalek rhetoric, as Americans made efforts to explore the continent, draw and defend boundaries, and situate themselves as the dominant power in North America.[22]

More recently, the rhetoric of Amalek was used by some Hutu preachers in Rwanda to justify the genocide of Tutsi people there in 1994,[23] and it was invoked by U.S. preacher John MacArthur to justify

---

[22] John Corrigan, "Amalek and the Rhetoric of Extermination," in Chris Benek and Christopher S. Grenda, eds., *The First Prejudice: Religious Tolerance and Intolerance in Early America* (Philadelphia: University of Pennsylvania Press, 2011), 70–71.

[23] Gerard van 't Spijker, "Focused on Reconciliation: Rwandan Protestant Theology After the Genocide," *Transformation* 34, no. 1, 2017, 66–74, https://www.jstor.org/stable/90008946.

the U.S. invasion of Iraq.[24] Theology can be deadly, and Winthrop's speech no longer seems so shining after all. And let's not forget that the Massachusetts Bay Colony Winthrop helped establish and lead was a Christian Nationalist state that used coercive state power to demand religious conformity. The religious dissenters banished from the colony included Puritan minister John Wheelwright, Anne Hutchinson, and Roger Williams (who later founded Rhode Island and cofounded the first Baptist church in America). Others were executed, like Mary Dyer, William Robinson, and Marmaduke Stephenson, for being Quakers.

Interestingly, Winthrop's line about America being the "city upon a hill" was largely ignored for more than three centuries. It received a few references, such as in a speech by President-elect John F. Kennedy in 1961, but didn't really enter the popular political imagination until Ronald Reagan won the presidency in 1980. Reagan is also the one who edited the text a bit to cast America not merely as a "city upon a hill" but a "shining city upon a hill." Conservative historian Richard M. Gamble argued in his book *In Search of the City on a Hill* that Reagan really "invented" the way the "city on a hill" metaphor is used today in U.S. politics as he took it beyond what Jesus and even Winthrop meant. Gamble added:

> More than any other modern figure, Reagan transformed Jesus's metaphor into a political slogan inseparable from the 1980s 'Reagan Revolution' and from that movement's legacy in the Republican Party. ... Its political use has been potent enough to all but eclipse its biblical meaning, even among American Christians who might reasonably be expected to resent seeing their metaphor dressed up like Uncle Sam.[25]

The political meaning eclipsed the biblical meaning ... of a Bible verse! If that's not a sign something's amiss, then nothing will wake us up.

---

[24] Robert Parham, "What Would Jesus Do About War with Iraq?" *Ethics Daily*, March 14, 2003, https://gfmarchives.com/what-would-jesus-do-about-war-with-iraq-cms-2300.

[25] Richard M. Gamble, *In Search of the City on a Hill: The Making and Unmaking of an American Myth* (New York: Continuum International Publishing Group, 2012), 143.

Unfortunately, it's not the only way the red letters of Jesus (and the black letters of the rest of scripture) are recast in red, white, and blue.

American Idol

As Benny Tate proved with his prayer during a U.S. House session, the "city upon a hill" passage is far from the only verse refashioned as if about the United States. Several others frequently show up in Christian Nationalist prayers and speeches. Most of all, 2 Chronicles 7:14 (or is it "Two Chronicles"?). It was the most-cited verse during prayers at Trump campaign rallies leading up to the 2024 election.[26] It's also commonly used with Christian Nationalist events like the National Day of Prayer. And at first glance, it makes sense why.

"If my people who are called by my name humble themselves, pray, seek my face, and turn from their wicked ways, then I will hear from heaven, and will forgive their sin and heal their land," we read in the text.

The biggest danger here is in redefining "my people." Who are God's people? Is it those who follow God, or is it people who are citizens of the United States? Conflating the two remains a key Christian Nationalist error. As Russell Moore, a longtime conservative evangelical leader, warned about such usage of the verse: "2 Chronicles 7:14 isn't about American politics."[27] He explained that while the verse is common in "God and country" messages, especially around the Fourth of July and Memorial Day, applying it to the U.S. ignores the context of the passage. It's written to people returning home from exile after being defeated and enslaved by a foreign power. It's a reminder to those on the bottom that God is still with them, not a wave-the-flag-pep-rally chant for those in power of the global empire. And it's definitely not a MAGA call to return to some bygone "again" era of greatness with a healed land, especially

---

[26] Kaylor, "Prayers of the MAGA Faithful."
[27] Russell Moore, "2 Chronicles Isn't About American Politics," RussellMoore. com, January 14, 2016, https://www.russellmoore.com/2016/01/14/2-chronicles-714-isnt-about-american-politics.

given the racism, patriarchy, genocide, and more in America's past. Ultimately, applying the verse to the U.S. instead of to God's people makes an idol out of the nation.

"We too often see America as somehow more 'real' than the kingdom, and our country as more important than the church," Moore explained. "Let's instead define ourselves not by the generic god of American values. We do not serve that god. We serve the God of Abraham, and of Isaac, and of Jacob, the God and Father of Jesus Christ. The promises that he has made will outlast Mount Rushmore."

That's why Moore, a "Never Trump" conservative, has criticized Christian Nationalism not just for its political agenda but for its handling of the Bible. As he argued: "Christian Nationalism is not a politically enthusiastic version of Christianity, nor is it a religiously informed patriotism. Christian Nationalism is a prosperity gospel for nation-states, a liberation theology for White people."[28] Why he warned about such treatment of the Bible was on display during the 2024 Republican National Convention as one of the speakers, Sara Workman, invoked 2 Chronicles 7:14. She argued:

> We need God in our hearts and Donald Trump back in the White House. ... Donald Trump put me on this stage to show that he hears us, he sees us, and we are forgotten no more. I find peace in God's promise that says, "If my people, who are called by my name would humble themselves and pray, I will hear your nation." Amen. With faith, hope, and love in my heart, I know we will make America great again.[29]

A verse about reminding people they belong to God and God is with them instead became a partisan pitch for electing a particular candidate to make a nation great. Adding to the conflation, she even subtly changed the wording of the verse (an issue we'll address more fully in chapter 8) by speaking not of "their land" but "our nation." Such a name-it-and-claim-it theology strips the passage out of its ancient

---

[28] Russell Moore, *Losing Our Religion: An Altar Call for Evangelical America* (New York: Sentinel, 2023), 117.

[29] Watch the clip: Brian Kaylor (@BrianKaylor), X, July 15, 2024, https://x.com/BrianKaylor/status/1813006307407921581.

context to make it about a modern nation-state, a concept completely foreign to the original audience.

In a similar vein, Neal Jackson, a Baptist pastor and state lawmaker in North Carolina, invoked both Psalm 33:12 and Joshua 1:9 to apply to the United States during his prayer at the RNC:

> Heavenly Father, we thank you for the blessings upon the United States of America. Thank you for your provisions upon this land, your protection of this land, and your promotion of this land which is undeniable. Your word says, "Blessed is the nation whose God is the Lord." Tonight, we claim that for America, believing that you desire to bless and prosper our country as we honor you and your ways. … Tonight, we pray for our military leaders and officers, pray for our police officers, our firefighters, our first responders as they risk their lives so that we can continue to be the land of the free and the home of the brave. You commanded Joshua to "be strong and courageous." Tonight, all across this country, I pray that you would raise up a generation of courageous leaders who follow you in their whole heart and govern with integrity.[30]

Again, the focus of the biblical citations was to push people to trust more in a nation than in God. Not to be outdone, South Dakota Gov. Kristi Noem went to the RNC podium and dragged 2 Timothy 1:7 out to a gravel pit and shot it (yes, that incident continues to dog her[31]). After quoting from Abraham Lincoln's Gettysburg Address, she linked that to Trump and Paul to encourage the delegates to keep fighting for America: "Like Lincoln in the midst of our pain and division, Donald Trump is calling us to be touched by the better angels of our nature. As Paul wrote in 2 Timothy, 'God has not given us a spirit of fear, but of power and of love and a sound mind.' We must not be afraid. Even in our darkest days we have never once given up hope, so don't quit

---

[30] Watch the clip: Brian Kaylor (@BrianKaylor), X, July 16, 2024, https://x.com/BrianKaylor/status/1813337330536915281.

[31] In case you forgot, she bragged in a memoir about taking a poorly trained puppy and killing it, barely getting the job done before her children got home from school to witness the slaughter.

on America."[32] The governor—later Trump's secretary of homeland security (look out immigrant puppies!)—essentially grabbed a random Bible verse to christen her argument that they should prove they love America by voting for Trump—which conjures up my favorite Bible verse to memorize as a child: John 11:35.[33]

Such use of the Bible matches what Bradley Onishi, a religion scholar and host of the popular *Straight White American Jesus* podcast, has noted as dangerous. The author of *Preparing for War: The Extremist History of White Christian Nationalism—And What Comes Next*, Onishi told me that when Christian Nationalists read the Bible, they do so with a couple of assumptions. The first is they assume "the United States is front and center in everything." This leads to a second assumption: "When it comes to the kingdom of God, the United States is at the center of that. So when they read the Bible, they're thinking about the United States. And then the assumption is we're the good guys. 'The only way you can stop a bad guy with a gun is a good guy with a gun.' The foundational idea is that we are always the good guys." This comes with an embrace of violent as righteous (as we'll unpack more in the next chapter). But it also works to disciple believers to confuse the focus of our faith, replacing God and God's kingdom with the president and the United States. As Andrew Whitehead, a leading scholar of Christian Nationalism, warned in his book *American Idolatry*, Christian Nationalism "betrays the gospel." He added:

> White Christian Nationalism creates disciples who are more concerned with advancing their own kingdom of this world through acquiring and defending self-interested power than with advancing the kingdom of God through service—a kingdom where everyone can flourish. Instead of being willing to serve for the sake of the King, Christian Nationalism demands we amass power over others for the sake of an earthly kingdom that benefits only "us." ... Instead of proclaiming all

---

[32] Watch the clip: Brian Kaylor (@BrianKaylor), X, July 15, 2024, https://x.com/BrianKaylor/status/1813021257555976203.
[33] In case Kristi Noem is reading, the full verse is: "Jesus wept."

humans as image-bearers and listening to how we can work toward a collective prosperity, White Christian Nationalism elevates some as favored and blessed by God above others.[34]

Whitehead added that Christian Nationalism glorifies power, fear, and violence to the point that it "produces Christians who bear little resemblance to a Savior who, being in the very nature of God, humbled himself, made himself nothing, becoming a servant to all."[35] It's often said that "you are what you eat." More profoundly, we become what we worship. We take on the values of what we glorify. A Bible recast in red, white, and blue is one holey Bible that leads us to fly the wrong flag.

Confusing the Community

I found myself sitting inside the Missouri Baptist Convention headquarters amid the 2022 campaign. It's a brutalist-style building—think tons of concrete and odd shapes like the FBI building and lots of Soviet-era structures. But all the windows were long ago covered up on the outside (since Brutalist buildings don't usually include many windows), so it's just a seven-story structure of vertical concrete lines for state Southern Baptist leaders to gather in like a secretive cult hidden from the rest of the world (metaphor alert?). My mother actually worked there a couple of years before being wrongly fired as retaliation for accusing the MBC leader of sexual harassment and gender discrimination (and the MBC a few years later eventually admitted he was behaving improperly and fired him). So entering the building is a bit weird for me. Even more so to join a private lunch event by a Christian Nationalist group trying to get conservative pastors and other church leaders to run for political office.

The group behind the event, American Renewal Project, was started by longtime Religious Right organizer David Lane. Although not a household name, he's been praised as a friend by numerous politicians, like U.S. Sen. Ted Cruz. His son Jackson worked with the

---

[34] Andrew L. Whitehead, *American Idolatry: How Christian Nationalism Betrays the Gospel and Threatens the Church* (Grand Rapids, MI: Brazos Press, 2023), 180.

[35] Whitehead, American Idolatry, 181.

2024 Trump campaign to recruit the pastors who prayed at campaign rallies, and Trump later named Jackson as the third-ranking official in the White House Faith Office led by Trump's longtime spiritual adviser, Paula White-Cain. The elder Lane's ARP focused on a few states in recent years, most notably North Carolina. For 2022, they claimed they recruited fifty pastors to run for office in North Carolina, with half of them winning their Republican primaries and ten winning in the general election. There, they worked closely with Lt. Gov. Mark Robinson, a controversial Christian Nationalist who lost his 2024 gubernatorial campaign amid scandals about pornography and using anti-Semitic and homophobic slurs. They've also worked with former Arkansas Gov. Mike Huckabee (a former Southern Baptist pastor who became U.S. ambassador to Israel in Trump's second term). In the MBC building, I heard from pastors from various states, including one from North Carolina who became a county commissioner and who in his remarks mixed in biblical passages about David killing Goliath and three Hebrews defying King Nebuchadnezzar along with anti-vax rhetoric, election denialism, and Christian Nationalism. Also speaking was former U.S. Attorney General John Ashcroft and his son, then-Missouri Secretary of State Jay Ashcroft, along with Texas pastor and future longshot presidential candidate Ryan Binkley.[36]

I signed up for the event, not sure they would let me in. Fortunately, the people in the MBC building weren't in charge and didn't seem to notice me. So I grabbed a complimentary Chick-fil-A lunch and a seat near the back to observe the Christian Nationalism along with some tasty peanut-oil-fried chicken, waffle fries, a chocolate chip cookie, and lemonade (who knew research could taste so good). There was a weird moment when I felt like I was in some sort of abstract art exhibit as we watched a video about ARP events in North Carolina. We saw clips from Robinson as well as some of the speakers there in the room with us. But as I took a bite of my chicken sandwich, I watched people on the screen eating Chick-fil-A while listening to David Lane—who was wearing the same outfit on the video as he was

---

[36] It's okay if you've not heard of him, he received just 774 votes in the Iowa caucuses (0.7%) and 315 in the New Hampshire primary (0.1%) despite spending more than $8 million on his campaign after saying God told him to run.

while sitting at the table in front of me. There was something oddly performative about the whole exercise. And the rhetoric matched. I heard about how we were called "for such a time as this," that we should not submit to government authority on public health measures, and that the U.S. was intended to be led by Christians.

"There's no such thing as the separation of church and state," Lane declared in the video shown at our event. "The First Amendment is to keep the state out of the church. I mean, my goal is to restore America to our Judeo-Christian heritage and re-establish a biblically based culture."

The idea of a "Judeo-Christian heritage" is a political talking point to seem inclusive. But that event could not be called Jewish; it was explicitly Christian and about getting Christians to govern. And the idea of a one-way wall of separation only to keep the state out of the church is absurd. A one-way wall doesn't exist. If you knock a hole in the wall next to you, it won't just let you go into the next room but will also let anyone there enter your room. Lane needs to tear down that wall in order to accomplish his mission of remaking the U.S. into a "Christian" nation. He also has to reframe biblical teachings. A key argument he and others with ARP make is that the Greek word usually translated as "church" in the New Testament—*ekklesia*—isn't really a religious gathering but rather a political term about ruling the community. That means Christians should head into the political sphere and dominate. That's why, Lane explained, he's "trying to push spiritual leaders into the public square based upon Jesus's Kingdom assignment from Matthew 16:18, when he said to Peter, 'On this rock, I will build my *ekklesia.*'"[37] An ARP leader emphasized that argument in the MBC building, saying that the *ekklesia* was "where the government of the community was stationed" and "we're called to be the *ekklesia.*" This is not an original argument, nor is it completely made up. It is true that the New Testament writers borrowed a Greek

---

[37] Jon Brown, "Activist Helping Pastors Win Elections Urges Christians to Have a 'Footprint in the Culture,'" *Christian Post*, February 26, 2024, https://www.christianpost.com/news/david-lane-urges-christians-to-get-involved-in-politics.html.

word about a political assembly to describe the new gathering of Jesus's followers, using the term over one hundred times. But that was a metaphor describing this alternative kingdom, not a call to take over the political kingdoms of the world.

To read Matthew 16 or other passages as a call for Christians to rule the political structures of their communities and the broader empire is to make the same error as Gov. Pontius Pilate when quizzing Jesus. Even after Jesus explained that "my kingdom is not of this world" and "my kingdom is from another place," Pilate couldn't get it, eventually scoffing, "What is truth?"[38] Then the people voted not for Jesus but for Barabbas, a man who tried to take power through a violent insurrection. At an event promoting the separation of church and state, Lutheran minister and journalist Angela Denker said she likes to point to the Jesus-Pilate conversation when talking to Christian Nationalists since the movement today "is but our most recent chapter of an ancient story of what happens when Christianity is co-opted by empire."[39] Yet, in contrast to what Jesus offered in that conversation with Pilate and on the cross, Denker lamented that today many are being discipled "by this dominant culture in America that paints God and paints Jesus as a muscular, violent, greedy, White man." That is, many people pushing Christian Nationalism want a messiah who looks more like Barabbas, one who's willing to take over and rule (including by force if necessary). They want a strongman to govern and help them in a quest toward baptizing America and codifying their interpretations of the Bible for everyone else. But it never works. America is not a Christian nation—not just because our founders really did create a radical experiment by separating church and state, but also because the modern nation-state never could be truly "Christian." Thus, America is not more blessed or loved by God than other nations. The hope of the world is not America; it's Jesus. The salt and light for the world is not America; it's Jesus's followers. And that's good news for everyone, except those who pledge allegiance to the empire.

---

[38] In case David Lane is reading, that's John 18:33–40.

[39] Brian Kaylor, "Supporting Church-State Separation with Faithful Challenges to Christian Nationalism," *A Public Witness*, April 10, 2025, https://publicwitness.wordandway.org/p/supporting-church-state-separation.

Steps Toward Not Misreading the Bible Like a Christian Nationalist

1. Avoid the temptation to read biblical passages as specially about the United States (or any other modern nation-state).
2. Watch out for when people take a passage about God's followers, disciples, or Church and instead apply it to another group like a nation or political party.
3. Read and listen to Christians from other nations, and, if possible, travel to visit them. Broadening our viewpoint beyond human-made borders is key to expanding our reading of scripture.

CHAPTER 7

The Bible as Warfare

Christian Nationalist preachers have christened Donald Trump as a reincarnation of numerous biblical heroes. He's a modern Cyrus, a new David, a contemporary Esther, and an updated messiah. Each of these comparisons bring their own hermeneutical errors and unique application problems. Comparing Trump to Cyrus (a godless king whom God uses) is quite different than calling him David (a chosen king after God's own heart) or a messianic leader to save the nation. Late in the 2024 presidential campaign, we saw a spike in another sloppy paint-by-numbers effort to depict Trump as a biblical hero. And this one highlighted a key problem with how Christian Nationalists read and apply the Bible: as a textbook for war.

"God has a prophetic destiny for America," charismatic "prophet" Herman Martir said before pointing to Trump's survival of an assassination attempt in July as proof that "God has his hand" on Trump. "I think we're at that moment where God is raising up to say, he is like that anointing, that Jehu anointing on him and is called by God to destroy Jezebel. ... This is spiritual warfare to the highest level and we need a war president."[1]

Martir, who has met with Trump multiple times and spoken at Lance Wallnau's "Courage Tour," made his comments on the

---
[1] Steve Shultz, "President Trump and the Jehu Anointing—Herman Martir," *Elijah Streams*, October 3, 2024, https://elijahstreams.com/videos/president-trump-and-the-jehu-anointing-herman-martir.

influential Christian Nationalist daily podcast *Elijah Streams*, whose guest list is basically a "Who's Who" of Christian Nationalists. In addition to various "prophets" like Ché Ahn, Dutch Sheets, Lou Engle, Kent Christmas, Cindy Jacobs, Jenny Donnelly, and Amanda Grace, the show has featured now-FBI Director Kash Patel, Eric Trump, Lara Trump, Michael Flynn, political trickster Roger Stone, and Dog the Bounty Hunter. So as much as I'd like to call the show and the comments on it fringe, it unfortunately is well-connected to leading Christian Nationalist preachers and politicians. And the comparison to Trump as a new Jehu wasn't unique to Martir and host Steve Shultz.

During an October 2024 rally called "A Million Women: An Esther Call to the Mall" (mentioned in chapter 5), "prophet" Ché Ahn made the Jehu comparison. Ahn had spoken previously at "Stop the Steal" rallies after the 2020 election and was in D.C. to support Trump on January 6, 2021. At the 2024 rally, he declared that he had come to make "an apostolic decree" with the U.S. Capitol behind him: "Trump is a type of Jehu, and Kamala Harris is a type of Jezebel. As you know, Jehu cast out Jezebel."[2] At that same event, Messianic Rabbi Jonathan Cahn, who converted from Judaism to Christianity and now preaches an end times-focused culture war gospel, took a sledgehammer to destroy an "altar to Ishtar" (a Mesopotamian goddess who isn't mentioned in the Bible but whom charismatic preachers have linked Jezebel to). People screamed and blew shofars as he struggled to beat it apart. Now, to be clear, that means to set up for the theatrical destruction of an altar, these Trumpian preachers literally built an altar to a false god! If only there was something in the Bible against building altars to false gods.

Cahn, who has compared Trump to Jehu since shortly after Trump's first election[3] and spoke at religious "Stop the Steal" rallies ahead of the insurrection, is probably the person most responsible for the Jehu rhetoric about Trump. He intensified the rhetoric in the days

---

[2] UPPERROOM, "A Million Women Event—Live in D.C.," YouTube, October 12, 2024, https://www.youtube.com/watch?v=FmTtIUcO4Bk&t.

[3] Sam Kestenbaum, "#MAGA Church: The Doomsday Prophet Who Says the Bible Predicted Trump," *New York Times*, March 15, 2019, https://www.nytimes.com/2019/03/15/nyregion/trump-preacher-magachurch.html.

leading up to the 2024 election. During a gathering of the Trump-backing National Faith Advisory Board just a couple of weeks before the election, Cahn declared:

> President Trump, you were born into the world to be a trumpet of God. ... God called you to walk according to the template, he called you according to the template of Jehu the warrior king. He called Jehu to make his nation great again. Jehu came to the capital city with an agenda to drain the swamp. Jehu forged an alliance with the religious conservatives of the land. So it was your destiny to do the same. To come to power, Jehu had to prevail against the nation's former first lady. ... Before you were born, God ordained that you would walk into his destiny and that if he should now bring you to the height of power, it will be for his glory. It will be the last act and maybe America's last chance of redemption.[4]

After Trump's inauguration in 2025, Cahn preached at his church a sermon titled "The Return of Jehu"[5] about how God removes and installs kings (which begs the question of why Cahn was fighting God's will by trying to overturn the 2020 election). As he preached in between showing clips from Trump's inauguration address (like it was the text for the message), Cahn tried to prove the Trump-Jehu comparison. He argued that "when Jehu came to power, he came in like a storm" and read a Bible commentary that used the word "stormed" to describe Jehu (the actual biblical texts do not use the word to describe Jehu). He then put on the church's screen the front page of *The New York Times* after Trump's 2024 victory with the big headline: "Trump Storms Back." Either I'm dead inside and the Spirit didn't move when I saw that, or Cahn is full of crap. If you've read this far, I assume you join me in the latter opinion. I'm pretty sure

---

[4] Daystar, "Rabbi Jonathan Cahn Released This Prophetic Message Over President Trump," YouTube, November 4, 2024, https://www.youtube.com/watch?v=JEWdq0yGJgc.

[5] Johnathan Cahn Official, "The Return of Trump: The Mystery & the Future," YouTube, January 28, 2025, https://www.youtube.com/watch?v=tK8rNwQ2Vzs.

that whatever adjective a newspaper used that day to describe Trump's return to power we could also find some commentary somewhere using that same word to describe Jehu or just about any major figure in the Bible. "Pharoah stormed at Moses," thus Trump is Pharoah. "Satan stormed heaven," ergo Trump is Satan. See how easy (and dumb) it is! Yet, Cahn thinks it's magical that *The Times* used "that Jehu word" to describe Trump. Cahn similarly found commentaries using words like "purge" and "dismantle" to describe Jehu's reign and compared that to headlines using those words for Trump. Cahn also noted the phrase "the sword of Jehu" in the Bible and then showed a picture of Trump holding a sword at an inaugural ball (which he had used to ceremonially cut a cake before awkwardly dancing and swinging the sword around). Interestingly, Cahn cropped the image so you can't see Vice President J.D. Vance also holding a sword since that might prove that just holding a sword doesn't make one Jehu. This approach to biblical interpretation is basically what you'd expect from someone wearing a tinfoil hat and cutting random words out of newspapers to tack on a wall with lots of strings, but Cahn is a popular figure at charismatic and political events and has prayed over Trump at Mar-a-Lago.

Such rhetoric isn't innocent. In the biblical story, Jehu didn't just take the throne from Jezebel in a nice, civil election. He conspired against the king, killed the king and others in a bloody insurrection, and ordered Jezebel to be thrown from the window where her body was mostly consumed by dogs. Once in power, Jehu ordered the slaughter of the children of Jezebel and had their heads piled at the city gate, and ordered the murders of other political and religious opponents. *The word of the Lord … thanks be to God!*

Such metaphors are dangerous, especially when employed by people who already supported a violent insurrection attempt. They see their side as righteously ordained by God to win, even if it requires killing those on the other side because this is about God's will for the nation. In the context of a political campaign that had already seen violence against those on both sides, this was pouring biblical gasoline on an open fire. Matthew Taylor, a religious studies scholar and author of *The Violent Take It by Force: The Christian Movement That Is Threatening Our Democracy*, denounced the Jehu-Jezebel rhetoric against Harris during the 2024 campaign as something that "verges on a threat on her life." He added:

> One of the most brutal and vindictive scenes in the Bible, Jehu's vengeance is being offered as the divinely ordained template for a second Trump term. ... Casting Trump as a Jehu creates theological permission for Christians to embrace Trump's promised violence. If he wins in this election, the Jehu image tells Trump's Christian supporters that some real-world violence may be needed to purge America of her demons.[6]

There are lots of biblical leaders and even kings that Christian Nationalist preachers could've chosen to justify their support of Trump. That many of them rallied around the biblical king with perhaps the most violent rise to power and one of the bloodiest reigns with purges of internal opponents is alarming. They are sanctifying violence and blessing authoritarian ambitions. And they do so ironically by failing to even read the whole passage. As we find at the end of Jehu's reign: "But Jehu was not careful to follow the law of the Lord the God of Israel with all his heart; he did not turn from the sins of Jeroboam, which he caused Israel to commit."[7] He's an evil, ungodly king!

Taking Off the Armor of God[8]

As more than three thousand people gathered under a revival tent at a church in Batavia, New York, multiple speakers insisted they were ready to fight. The rhetoric came during an installment of the

---

[6] Matthew D. Taylor, "Once a Beneficent King Cyrus, Trump Has Lately Been Cast as a Biblical Avenger," *Religion News Service*, November 1, 2024, https://religionnews.com/2024/11/01/once-a-beneficent-king-cyrus-trump-has-lately-been-cast-as-a-biblical-avenger.

[7] In case Ahn or Cahn are reading, that's 2 Kings 10:31.

[8] Part of this section is drawn from a piece cowritten with Beau Underwood and is used here with permission: Brian Kaylor and Beau Underwood, "Taking Off the Armor of God," *A Public Witness*, August 16, 2022, https://publicwitness.wordandway.org/p/taking-off-the-armor-of-god.

ReAwaken America Tour (or RAT for short), a series of events full of Christian Nationalism, anti-vax falsehoods, and election conspiracies headlined by Michael Flynn, Roger Stone, Eric Trump, pillow-hugger Mike Lindell, and numerous preachers and political activists. Paul Doyle, pastor of the church hosting the event, framed the movement in militaristic terms. Invoking the Civil War, he announced they were in "a battle of good and evil."[9] Doyle added, "Jesus bloodied himself for me, and I am ready to bloody myself for him."

Other speakers also used violent rhetoric, like Tennessee preacher Greg Locke, a regular at RAT events who rose to fame by fighting COVID-19 public health measures and from his presence in Washington, D.C., on January 6, 2021[10] (and who, as we saw in chapter 2, duct-taped a Bible to a baseball bat). He declared to applause:

> We so believe in our First Amendment right that if you show up on our campus and you try to shut us down with our First Amendment right, I said the boys will meet you at the door with our Second Amendment right because we are not playing your Democrat games. ... It's time we stand, having done all to stand because the weapons of our warfare are not carnal but mighty through God to the pulling down of strongholds. We better suit up, we better boot up, we better put on the whole armor of God because this ain't a circus, this is a war that we're in. This is a war that we're in.

Eric Trump came on stage shortly after Locke, endorsed the message, and encouraged more pastors to be like Locke. Trump added, "I like any pastor that's pro-Second Amendment. ... And I sure as hell like any pastor who's pro-Trump, and you are certainly pro-Trump. So Pastor Locke is my guy."

---

[9] Thrivetime Show, "ReAwaken America Tour—Batavia—Day 1," Rumble, August 12, 2022, https://rumble.com/v1fq0yv-reawaken-america-tour-batavia-day-1.html.

[10] Andy Humbles and Liam Adams, "The Evolution of Greg Locke: How a Controversial Tennessee Pastor Wants to Save America from Its Demons," *Nashville Tennessean*, April 20, 2022, https://www.tennessean.com/story/news/religion/2022/04/21/greg-locke-how-controversial-jan-6-pastor-wants-save-america/7208072001.

Locke wasn't the only RAT speaker over that weekend to cite the Ephesians 6:10–19 passage about the "armor of God" (which he mixed with 2 Corinthians 10:4). Pastor David Scarlett and "prophet" Amanda Grace regularly opened RAT events with the blowing of shofars to bring the Holy Spirit in (and despite all the times they've done this, they still haven't figured out how to make it a joyful noise). Later in the Batavia event, they read through and offered a verse-by-verse exposition of the Ephesians passage about the armor because, as Scarlett put it, "we're under warfare" and "it's offense time." Grace (not living up to her name) added that if they go on offense then "you are going to see major change in this country and you are going to see the wicked fall."

Such "armor of God" rhetoric is common at the RAT events, including the one I attended in Branson, Missouri, and others I've watched online. It's also a popular verse at other Christian Nationalist events. At RAT events and others, this rhetoric appears on stage along with cheering for people arrested for their roles in the January 6, 2021, insurrection—which is an unsurprising mix. As a report by the Baptist Joint Committee for Religious Liberty and the Freedom From Religion Foundation documented, some insurrectionists wore an "Armor of God" patch with a large cross on their camouflage fatigues.[11] Another insurrectionist wore a T-shirt in his mugshot that said "Armor of God" on top of a shield and two swords (one more sword than is actually in the passage). Meanwhile, politicians who tried to overturn the election also cited the passage. Like Mark Finchem, a member of the far-right militia the Oath Keepers, who was in Washington, D.C., on January 6 while a member of the Arizona House of Representatives (and in 2024 he won a seat to the state Senate). During a legislative hearing in late 2020, as he pushed false election claims as a state lawmaker to overturn Biden's win in the Grand Canyon State, Finchem invoked the Ephesians passage.

---

[11] Andrew L. Seidel, "Events, People, and Networks Leading up to January 6," in *Christian Nationalism and the January 6, 2021 Insurrection*, BJC, https://bjconline.org/wp-content/uploads/2022/02/Christian_Nationalism_and_the_Jan6_Insurrection-2-9-22.pdf.

"Ladies and gentleman, this is a skirmish," he declared. "You ain't seen nothing yet. Because when Satan wants to extinguish a light, he will stop at nothing. So be on your guard, put on the full armor of God, and be prepared to fight."[12]

Other politicians have also invoked the biblical passage to frame their politics, especially those who, like Finchem, supported efforts to overturn the 2020 presidential election that climaxed in the deadly insurrection, including:

- Darren Bailey, the Republican nominee for governor of Illinois in 2022, featured the biblical citation to the Ephesians passage on the door of his campaign bus like it was a campaign slogan.[13]
- Then-North Carolina Lt. Gov. Mark Robinson claimed in 2022 that Christians are "called to be led by men," so men must "put on the whole armor of God" and "take the head of your enemy in God's name."[14] During his failed gubernatorial campaign in 2024, Robison declared during a campaign stop in a Sunday church service: "Some folks need killing."[15]
- As Republican U.S. Rep. Lauren Boebert of Colorado answered a question about how she handled criticism from Democrats, she responded, "I have the armor of God, and that is all forward-facing to help me in the battle. I have the helmet of salvation, and the shield of faith, and the breast-

---

[12] Laurie Roberts, "Mark Finchem for Secretary of State? Michelle Ugenti-Rita? Is This a Joke?" *Arizona Republic*, May 27, 2021, https://www.azcentral.com/story/opinion/op-ed/laurieroberts/2021/05/27/republican-secretary-state-candidates-finchem-ugenti-rita-appalling/7475834002.

[13] Brian Kaylor and Beau Underwood, "Democrats Boosting Christian Nationalism," *A Public Witness*, June 28, 2022, https://publicwitness.wordandway.org/p/democrats-boosting-christian-nationalism.

[14] Travis Fain, "NC's Lieutenant Governor: 'We Are Called to Be 'Led by Men,' Not Women," WRAL, June 6, 2022, https://www.wral.com/nc-s-lieutenant-governor-we-are-called-to-be-led-by-men-not-women/20318578.

[15] Greg Sargent, "MAGA Gov. Candidate's Ugly, Hateful Rant: 'Some Folks Need Killing!'" *The New Republic*, July 5, 2024, https://newrepublic.com/article/183443/mark-robinson-north-carolina-gov-candidate-hateful-rant-killing.

plate of righteousness, the belt of truth, and the sword of the spirit, the shoes of peace. That's all forward-facing for the battle. So I am well armed to go into this battle."[16]

- After the FBI searched one of Trump's homes in 2022 and removed a variety of sensitive and classified documents that he improperly possessed, U.S. Rep. Matt Gaetz told Steve Bannon that Republicans "are ready for this battle" in response to the FBI search.[17] Gaetz added, "My assessment is the antidote has to be not one more damn penny for this administrative state that has been weaponized against our people in a very fascist way. ... We are ready for this battle. Let us put on the armor of God and go fight."

- Before becoming speaker of the House, Rep. Mike Johnson recorded a podcast episode at a Christian conference during Holy Week in 2022 in which he argued that in our "increasingly hostile culture" the Ephesians passage should trump teachings of Jesus (an issue we'll return to in chapter 8): "The kingdom of God allows aggression. ... 'Wait, I thought we were just supposed to turn the other cheek.' Well, there's a time to every purpose under heaven. There's a time for war. There's a time to every purpose under heaven. There is a time when you must stand up and contend for the faith. You have to defend. You have to fight for the truth. ... The armor of God, this is a very familiar passage to all of you."[18]

- As Kari Lake campaigned for the U.S. Senate in Arizona, she urged her supporters to literally arm themselves in the name of God: "We are going to put on the armor of God. Then

---

[16] Truth & Liberty, "Faith in God Repels Negative Attacks," Facebook, May 13, 2021, https://www.facebook.com/watch/?v=3583706701855474.

[17] Justin Horowitz, "Steve Bannon's Show Melts Down Over the FBI Search of Trump's Mar-a-Lago Residence," *Media Matters*, August 9, 2022, https://www.mediamatters.org/steve-bannon/steve-bannons-show-melts-down-over-fbi-search-trumps-mar-lago-residence.

[18] Mike Johnson and Kelly Johnson, "Episode 5: How Should Christians FIGHT?" *Truth Be Told*, Spotify, April 13, 2022, https://open.spotify.com/episode/0yAGYTW0RPcJSZEKMTGz5q.

maybe strap on a Glock on the side of us, just in case."[19] Her call to "strap on a Glock" not only showed an endorsement of political violence but also, ironically, suggested she doesn't believe the armor of God will actually work.

- After the failed assassination attempt on Trump, references to the passage erupted in part because of the timing (as explored in chapter 3). Others who didn't make the argument based on numerology also invoked the passage. Like Steve Bannon, who was in prison at the time for contempt of Congress: "I've warned about this very thing for over a year—an assassination attempt. The threat is real, very real. Thankfully, President Trump wears the armor of God."[20]
- As I found in an analysis of prayers at Trump campaign rallies for his 2024 campaign, the Ephesians 6 passage was the second-most popular passage (after 2 Chronicles 7:14)—and that was even true before the assassination attempt that elevated the "armor of God" passage.[21]

Politicians and preachers pushing Christian Nationalism keep citing Ephesians 6 to explain their efforts. But that's not what the passage actually teaches. Addressed to early Christians in the ancient city of Ephesus, the overarching focus of Ephesians is the Church's witness to the supremacy of God. The letter speaks to the triumph of God's reign known through the death and resurrection of Jesus Christ, while urging Christians to act accordingly as individuals and as a community of believers. Rather than supporting a political quest for power, one of the book's common threads is the need for Christians to stand fast in the face of imperial persecution. Their minority status within the empire put them at odds with the government,

---

[19] Molly Bohannon, "Kari Lake Tells Supporters to 'Strap on a Glock' in Preparation for 'Intense' Six Months," *Forbes*, April 16, 2024, https://www.forbes.com/sites/mollybohannon/2024/04/16/kari-lake-tells-supporters-to-strap-on-a-glock-in-preparation-for-intense-six-months/?sh=d133aafaca04.

[20] Jordan King, "Steve Bannon Reacts to Trump Shooting from Prison," *Newsweek*, July 15, 2024, https://www.newsweek.com/steve-bannon-donald-trump-shooting-assassination-attempt-1925173.

[21] Brian Kaylor, "Prayers of the MAGA Faithful," *A Public Witness*, January 9, 2024, https://publicwitness.wordandway.org/p/prayers-of-the-maga-faithful.

and sometimes even their own families. Ephesians 6 is not a call for beleaguered Christians to take up arms and seize control of the empire. Instead, it demands that the followers of God trust that God will provide for their defense amid the battles fought between spiritual forces.

"In the armed struggle with evil, the saints of God are on the defensive, not the offensive," New Testament scholar Richard Carlson explained. "This text is not an 'onward Christian soldiers' type of battle cry in which the church militant will usher in God's kingdom by attacking and rooting out all the forces which stand in opposition to God. Rather, the call is for the saints to stand firm and withstand the attacks of evil."[22]

The concern of Ephesians 6 is not the politics of any one nation; it is focused on the purity of the Church's testimony to the eternal victory of God. The passage promises God will act in defense of those who stand faithful and equip them with the armor necessary to endure evil's onslaught. It asks for trust in God's protection; it does not justify human aggression. Like those early believers in Ephesus, sincere Christians today face the challenge of remaining steadfast in their convictions despite these attempts by powerful leaders to undermine the claims of our faith and even to co-opt our sacred texts for Christian Nationalist power quests. Those in the public square citing Ephesians 6 about putting on the "armor of God" perceive themselves as in the middle of a fight or preparing for a war. They are not closely studying the biblical text to bolster their faith in a God who defends them against persecution by an empire. Christians must recognize that politicians and preachers using scripture in a militant quest for power disfigure the biblical witness to the reign of God. Their words reveal a refusal to flip over just a couple chapters and make "every effort to maintain the unity of the Spirit in the bond of peace" (Ephesians 4:3). So it's time for a moratorium on invoking the "armor of God" in partisan warfare. On that, I will stand my ground.

---

[22] Richard Carlson, "Commentary on Ephesians 6:10–20," *Working Preacher*, August 22, 2021, https://www.workingpreacher.org/commentaries/revised-common-lectionary/ordinary-21-2/commentary-on-ephesians-610-20-6.

Killer Bible Stories

Which biblical story someone employs as a metaphor today matters since, as linguist George Lakoff argued, "Metaphors can kill."[23] He explained that before a war begins, the nation's leaders often set the stage with the metaphors they use to describe the enemy. We've seen this in Nazi Germany, Rwanda before the genocide, and numerous other occasions. Using a violent lens like "Jehu" or the "armor of God" impacts how one sees the world and acts within it. In their book *Metaphors We Live By*, Lakoff and Mark Johnson insisted a "metaphor is not just a matter of language, that is, of mere words."[24] Rather, metaphors impact not just "how we perceive" and "how we think" but also "what we do."[25] Consider the difference Lakoff and Johnson offered between calling an argument "war" and calling it "dance." Even as a Baptist who doesn't really dance (more because I lack the ability than for morality reasons), I recognize the difference between the two metaphors. With the first metaphoric framework of a war, we "win or lose arguments" and "see the person we are arguing with as an opponent." It's all about winning because nothing else matters. With the second depiction of an argument as a dance, we see it as a place "where no one won or lost, where there was no sense of attacking or defending." The other person then is our partner as we both give and take to create something new and hopefully beautiful together. Simply changing our wording—and thus our view—of arguments from that of "war" to "dance" would drastically change how we act in arguments. As Lakoff and Johnson explained, people in these different worldviews "would view arguments differently, experience them differently, carry them out differently, and talk about them differently."[26]

The same is true when we start embracing biblical stories to describe ourselves and other people. Once we frame ourselves as divinely chosen violent biblical "heroes," then it's easier to support

---

[23] George Lakoff, *Don't Think of an Elephant* (White River Junction, VT: Chelsea Green Publishing, 2004), 69.
[24] George Lakoff and Mark Johnson, *Metaphors We Live By* (Chicago: University of Chicago Press, 1980), 6.
[25] Lakoff and Johnson, *Metaphors We Live By*, 4.
[26] Lakoff and Johnson, *Metaphors We Live By*, 5.

or even engage in actual violence. And as the January 6, 2021, insurrection proved, Christian Nationalism can be violent. During the push between the 2020 presidential election that Trump lost and the Capitol insurrection where his supporters tried to violently overturn the election, a number of "prophets" and religious leaders—like Ché Ahn, Jonathan Cahn, and Greg Locke—joined the so-called "Stop the Steal" movement. The most explicitly religious events were "Jericho March" rallies held in December and the week of the insurrection. The effort drew from the biblical story of how Joshua fit the battle of Jericho (Jericho, Jericho) by walking around it for seven days until the walls came tumblin' down.

A Jericho March event on December 12, 2020, featured the blowing of shofars and remarks by Lance Wallnau, Eric Metaxas, Michael Flynn, Mike Lindell, radio host Alex Jones (who denies the massacre at Sandy Hook occurred), Roger Stone, and a Catholic archbishop and priest who were both later defrocked for schismatic rhetoric. Another Jericho March was held on the eve of the insurrection in addition to daily marches around the Capitol and Supreme Court buildings in the days leading up to January 6. Writing for *The Atlantic* two days after the attack on the Capitol, reporter Emma Green pointed to the Jericho Marches as a key example of how January 6 was "a Christian insurrection" where "many of those who mobbed the Capitol on Wednesday claimed to be enacting God's will."[27] The organizers of the Jericho March events saw themselves as a new Joshua movement instructed by God to take the Promised Land (which I didn't realize was actually just a swamp flowing with bureaucrats and monuments). As a promotion for the Jericho March movement declared:

> Jericho was a city of false gods and corruption. On God's command, Joshua and the army of Israel marched around the city seven times and let out a loud shout, and God brought down the walls of the city and exposed the darkness. Our Jericho March was born of a vision from God. ... This is our battle of Jericho for people of faith and patriots from all

---

[27] Emma Green, "A Christian Insurrection," *The Atlantic*, January 8, 2021, https://www.theatlantic.com/politics/archive/2021/01/evangelicals-catholics-jericho-march-capitol/617591.

across America. We believe in a great and powerful God who can move mountains, expose corruption, and restore justice. We believe in a God of miracles.[28]

Speakers at the events built up the metaphor that they were there to tear down the walls of the "deep state" of Jericho so Trump could win and remain in office. Like Bishop Leon Benjamin, who spoke at the first Jericho March:

> Joshua is told to do something crazy, but we know when God tells us to do something crazy it means it's going to work. … You came to bring these Jericho walls down in Washington, D.C. … The demons we kill now, our children will not have to fight these devils. These are our devils, and we will kill them now. They will not fight our children. The Jericho walls must come down![29]

Yet, despite the violence we saw on January 6, preachers and politicians who pushed the election lies generally remain unrepentant. And many—like Ahn, Cahn, and Locke—continue to use violent biblical imagery. In addition to drawing on stories like David killing Goliath, Jehu killing Jezebel, and Paul describing the armor of God, other popular passages used include Isaiah 54:17 about how "no weapon that is fashioned against you shall prosper." In my analysis of prayers at Trump rallies during the 2024 campaign, it was the third-most popular passage after 2 Chronicles 7:14 and Ephesians 6:11.[30] It also came in as the fourth-most popular verse quoted during the 2024 Republican National Convention after Matthew 5:14 ("city on a hill"), Esther

---

[28] Peter Montgomery, "Right-Wing Religious and Political Activists Trying to Overturn Biden Victory Will Converge on Washington Dec. 12," *Right Wing Watch*, December 8, 2020, https://www.peoplefor.org/rightwingwatch/post/right-wing-religious-and-political-activists-trying-to-overturn-biden-victory-will-converge-on-washington-dec-12.

[29] Right Side Broadcasting, "Jericho March Live from Washington, DC," Facebook, December 12, 2020, https://www.facebook.com/rsbnetwork/videos/188101792958083.

[30] Kaylor, "Prayers of the MAGA Faithful."

4:14 ("such a time as this"), and Ephesians 6:11.[31] In its new political context, it came with a partisan and literal tinge alongside chants like "Fight! Fight! Fight!" Others like to cherry-pick Matthew 10:34, when Jesus said he did "not come to bring peace, but a sword," while ignoring Matthew 26:52, when he disarmed Peter and said that "all who take the sword will perish by the sword." The selective literalism of Christian Nationalists (as we saw in chapter 4) becomes even more problematic when coupled with a preference for violent texts.

Such support for violence can be seen in survey data, like when PRRI found in 2024 that "Christian Nationalists are about twice as likely as other Americans to believe political violence may be justified."[32] That's why Drew Strait, a New Testament professor at Anabaptist Mennonite Biblical Seminary and author of *Strange Worship: Six Steps for Challenging Christian Nationalism*, told me that "biblical interpretation is a human security studies issue" much like after the 9/11 terrorist attacks there was attention to security implications of differing interpretations of the Qur'an. He added:

> I absolutely love the Bible. I also, in the same breath, recognize that when read irresponsibly, the Bible has an extraordinary capacity to harm people, especially vulnerable people. And so the Bible is a dangerous book. … We need to think of biblical interpretation as a human security issue. How we interpret the Bible matters. Biblical interpretation can bring life to this world; it can also take life away from this world. And we have way more many examples of this throughout the history of interpretation than I wish we had.

When Christian Nationalists do violence to the text, it is sometimes just a pretext for literal violence against people. That's why we must challenge the dangerous abuses of scripture in our politics and pulpits today.

---

[31] Kelsey Dallas, "The Bible Verses in the Spotlight at Part Conventions," *Deseret News*, August 27, 2024, https://www.deseret.com/faith/2024/08/27/bible-verses-used-by-politicians.

[32] "Support for Christian Nationalism in All 50 States: Findings from PRRI's 2023 American Values Atlas," PRRI, February 28, 2024, https://www.prri.org/research/support-for-christian-nationalism-in-all-50-states.

Steps Toward Not Misreading the Bible Like a Christian Nationalist

1. Avoid the use of violent biblical metaphors and stories to describe your goals, and reject the use of such violent rhetoric when employed by others.
2. Be alert against overuse of the "armor of God" rhetoric, especially in ways to justify partisan political acts or that call people to literal fighting.
3. Reject any preacher or politician who paved the way for the January 6, 2021, insurrection, especially those who remain unrepentant and who used the Lord's name in vain by depicting the plot to overturn an election as a divine mission.

CHAPTER 8

The Bible as Rewritable

As Florida Gov. Ron DeSantis celebrated his official gubernatorial renomination in 2022, he decided to quote the Bible. Well, kind of. You won't quite find the verse articulated this way in any translation.

"I am calling on all Floridians to put on the full armor of God as we will fight tooth and nail to protect Florida from the destructive agenda of Joe Biden and his number one ally in Florida, Charlie Crist," the governor said.[1] "This state is worth fighting for, our country is worth fighting for. So put on the full armor of God and take a stand against the left's schemes."[2]

It's a line DeSantis clearly likes, as he used it at multiple other events to urge conservatives to prepare for a righteous battle. Like during a 2022 event sponsored by Trumpian activist Charlie Kirk's Turning Point USA: "Get ready for battle. Put on the full armor of God. Take a stand against the left's schemes. Stand firm with the belt of truth buckled around your waist. You will face flaming arrows, but the shield of faith will protect you. And so, in 2022, I think this

---

[1] Tim Craig and Lori Rozsa, "DeSantis Flexes Influence with 'Anti-Woke' School Board Victories," *Washington Post*, August 24, 2022, https://www.washingtonpost.com/nation/2022/08/24/florida-desantis-schools-election.

[2] "Incumbent Gov. Ron DeSantis (R-FL): 'So Put on the Full Armor of God and Take a Stand Against the Left's Schemes,'" *The Recount*, August 23, 2022, https://therecount.com/watch/incumbent-gov-ron-desantis-rfl/2645884669.

November is going to be the time when America fought back."[3] At another rally, the governor who had recently signed a bill limiting what public school teachers can say about sexuality declared, "Gird your loins for battle. We are going to fight. You put on the full armor of God. You take a stand against the left's schemes."[4]

He's used the line so many times that it's clearly not a verbal stumble. He's intentionally rewriting the text. As discussed in the previous chapter, the "armor of God" passage is a popular one amongst Christian Nationalists. But they usually at least quote it accurately. In the new revised DeSantis version, the devil is replaced with "the left." With that twist, he uses scripture to demonize—or, perhaps worse, devilize—his political opponents.

By rewriting the words of the Bible, DeSantis changed the meaning of the text. DeSantis baptized the Republican Party as the new church. He was not merely comparing "the left" to the devil; he was suggesting that liberals aren't really Christians. And he was arguing that Republicans are inherently righteous—not because they believe in Jesus but because they vote for candidates like himself. DeSantis redefined Christianity through the lens of partisan politics. Thus, he preached this new gospel not in churches but at campaign rallies as the GOP faithful applauded in devotion. Treating political opponents as agents of Lucifer threatens our democracy. But it's even more dangerous when scripture is rewritten to justify partisan politics and heretical theology. Sadly, his line kept drawing large applause at his partisan crowds, which helps explain why he kept using it. The Republican Party is neither the church nor an angelic host. For DeSantis to suggest otherwise weakens concerns about power and corruption. Anything his side does can be excused, even efforts to overturn a free and fair election. If he reads more of the Bible, DeSantis will learn that "all have sinned and fall short of the glory of God."[5] I checked my Bible, and there's no exception for DeSantis. Unfortunately, DeSantis isn't

---

[3] Brian Kaylor and Beau Underwood, "Taking Off the Armor of God," *A Public Witness*, August 16, 2022, https://publicwitness.wordandway.org/p/taking-off-the-armor-of-god.

[4] Kaylor and Underwood, "Taking Off the Armor of God."

[5] In case the governor is reading, that's Romans 3:23.

the only one to engage in blatant rewriting of scripture—nor is he the only one to gain applause with a new partisan translation. With Christian Nationalistic politicians rewriting the Bible to undermine our democracy and our faith, we need to prepare ourselves so we can stand against such schemes.

Challenging the 'Jezebel Spirit'

As Indiana's gubernatorial candidates squared off in a debate just a month before the 2024 election, Democratic nominee Jennifer McCormick repeatedly criticized her Republican opponent's running mate for accusing her of having a "Jezebel spirit." Micah Beckwith, a controversial pastor who upset state GOP leaders by capturing the lieutenant governor nomination, was running on a ticket with U.S. Sen. Mike Braun. As Braun and McCormick addressed various issues and took shots at each other, McCormick mentioned Beckwith's attacks on her. A Republican-turned-Democrat, McCormick was a former state superintendent of public instruction and a former public school administrator who had been married for nearly thirty years to a public school teacher. But to Beckwith, McCormick was the personification of an evil spirit.

"If you look at the Republican ticket versus the Democrat[ic] ticket, it's strength and godly boldness versus just I would say the Jezebel spirit and just this idea of no boldness or boldness for immorality," Beckwith said on a podcast pushing a fifty-day pre-election prayer effort.[6]

During her debate with Bruan, McCormick brought up Beckwith's comment along with the fact Braun's campaign was using an ad with a digitally altered image of her. She called the "Jezebel spirit" rhetoric "extremism" that's "beyond the Hoosier values," and she connected it to Beckwith calling himself a "Christian Nationalist."[7] She also pushed Braun to admit those attacks were wrong and apologize, but

---

[6] Right Wing Watch, "GOP Lt. Gov. Nominee Micah Beckwith Says Indiana Must Choose Between 'Godly Boldness' and Jezebel," YouTube, September 30, 2024, https://www.youtube.com/watch?v=-5RLaRNZP5o.

[7] The Political Spotlight, "Indiana's Two-Thirds Gubernatorial Debate," YouTube, October 2, 2024, https://www.youtube.com/live/Mhi8VMDksBE.

he refused to do so on either account. So McCormick questioned if Braun has the character needed to lead. The line of attack shouldn't have surprised Braun, as McCormick had already addressed it on social media. Noting how she was being called a "Jezebel spirit" despite her record as a wife, mom, teacher, and public servant, she added, "Ladies—we deserve better than this." [8]

While Beckwith claimed his "Jezebel spirit" attack had "nothing to do with being a woman or not," such attacks are usually used against women. Vice President Kamala Harris was also called a "Jezebel spirit," most notably by Trumpian "prophet" Lance Wallnau, a key figure in the New Apostolic Reformation (as covered in chapter 3). Shortly after Harris became the Democratic nominee, Wallnau argued the 2024 election was "Trump vs. the Jezebel spirit."[9] After pushing whey protein products for people to buy, he explained why he thought Trump would still win and why he thought Harris was a "Jezebel spirit."

"When you've got somebody operating in manipulation, intimidation, and domination—especially when it's in a female role trying to emasculate a man who is standing up for truth—you're dealing with the Jezebel spirit," Wallnau said. "So with Kamala, you have a Jezebel spirit, a characteristic in the Bible that is the personification of intimidation, seduction, domination, and manipulation."

Wallnau's actually been calling Harris "a Jezebel spirit" since 2020. But he increased the rhetoric after Harris became the Democratic presidential nominee in 2024. He insisted Harris represented "the spirit of Jezebel in a way that will be even more ominous than Hillary because she'll bring a racial component and she's younger."[10] Yet, of the two presidential candidates in 2024, Harris was the only one who was actually a member of a church.

While some journalists tried to point out the meaning of the "Jezebel spirit" comments by Beckwith and Wallnau, they often

---

[8] Jennifer McCormick (@McCormickForGov), X, October 1, 2024, https://x.com/mccormickforgov/status/1841075837270970821.

[9] Watch the full video: Lance Wallnau (@LanceWallnau), X, September 13, 2024, https://x.com/lancewallnau/status/1834767693922324491.

[10] Right Wing Watch (@RightWingWatch), X, July 22, 2024, https://x.com/RightWingWatch/status/1815392389558669479.

mixed up the details. Like an Indiana political publication that called the "Jezebel spirit" attack "a biblical phrase about wicked women."[11] There's just one problem: "Jezebel spirit" is *not* a biblical phrase.

Although the name Jezebel shows up twenty times in the Bible—in 1 Kings, 2 Kings, and Revelation—there is no use of the phrase "Jezebel spirit." Nineteen of the biblical uses of Jezebel refer to a queen of the northern kingdom of Ephraim after Israel split. The texts introduce her as a Phoenician princess, daughter of the King of Tyre (which is in modern-day Lebanon). She married King Ahab in the northern kingdom, who is generally regarded as one of the eviler kings ruling over that part of the Hebrew people. The texts blame her for pushing the worship of Baal, killing prophets of God, and stealing land after killing the people who owned it. The prophet Elijah condemned both Ahab and Jezebel. Eventually, Ahab and Jezebel both met a bloody ending. After Ahab died in battle, one son briefly ruled before dying and another son then ruled for twelve years. But the House of Ahab came to an end in a violent coup by Jehu. After killing the king and other family members, Jehu ordered servants to throw Jezebel from a window. Her body was then mostly eaten by stray dogs. (Such a great story for children's time next Sunday!)

There is one additional Jezebel reference in the Book of Revelation. In the letter to the church in Thyatira, condemnation is given for tolerating "that woman Jezebel, who calls herself a prophet" (some translations say "your wife Jezebel"). Many scholars and preachers argue this wasn't really the woman's name but that she's being compared to the ancient queen. That might be true, though they don't point to textual evidence of "Jezebel" being used as such an insult yet. The reasoning for the argument that Jezebel is not her real name is that no one would name their daughter after that evil queen. But people literally name their daughters Jezebel today even after the Revelation text further poisoned the name's connotations. Sure, it's only about twenty babies out of a million in the U.S. today, according to Social

---

[11] Leslie Bonilla Muñiz, "Democrat Group Pumps $600,000 into Indiana Governor Race as Analysts Revise Forecasted Result," *Indiana Capital Chronicle*, October 4, 2024, https://indianacapitalchronicle.com/briefs/democrat-group-pumps-600000-into-indiana-governor-race-as-analysts-revise-forecasted-result.

Security Administration data, but it happens. Other people portrayed as villains in the biblical texts—like Delilah and Cain—also still get picked sometimes as names today.

It is the Revelation 2:20 reference that particularly adds to the connotations of Jezebel today since that woman is not only described as a false prophet but also as one pushing sexual immorality. (She was also criticized for pushing the eating of food that had been sacrificed to idols, but Paul also said that was okay.) Whether the woman was actually named Jezebel or just called that in the verse, there's still no reference in the Bible to a "Jezebel spirit."

The use of "Jezebel" as an insult against women is not new. The term has especially been used against Black women since the time of slavery to claim they were hypersexual. This was used to justify the raping of enslaved women by arguing they actually wanted it. The racist and sexist trope continued during Jim Crow and beyond. As Kamala Harris put her hand on a Bible to take the vice-presidential oath of office in 2021, multiple Southern Baptist pastors sparked national controversy for calling Harris a "Jezebel."[12] Rev. Amos C. Brown, a civil rights icon and Harris's longtime pastor, penned a *Word&Way* column at the time in response to the "Jezebel" attacks on Harris.

"For a White man to use that word to describe any Black woman is demeaning in the extreme," Brown wrote. "Such vile tropes have no place in our society or political discourse."[13]

While the term "Jezebel" has long been used as an attack line, the idea of a "Jezebel spirit" didn't gain popularity until much more recently. I searched Google's analysis of books published since 1800 and found that the phrase "Jezebel spirit" was virtually unused until the early 1990s. From 1994–2001 it rose dramatically—and is now at its highest recorded level. So what happened? Some hints of the embrace of this phrase can be seen in books starting to use the phrase around that time.

---

[12] Brian Kaylor, "Calvinist Group Defends 'Jezebel' Attack on VP Kamala Harris," *Word&Way*, February 14, 2021, https://wordandway.org/2021/02/14/calvinist-group-defends-jezebel-attacks-on-vp-kamala-harris.

[13] Amos C. Brown, "The First Step to Reconciliation," *Word&Way*, February 9, 2021, https://wordandway.org/2021/02/09/the-first-step-to-reconciliation.

Charismatic preacher Bill Hamon, an "apostle" in the New Apostolic Reformation movement, referenced the "Jezebel spirit" in his 1991 book *Prophets, Pitfalls, and Principles: God's Prophetic People Today*. In 1994, Francis Frangipane, who started a charismatic ministry in Iowa, published *The Jezebel Spirit*. The same year, Bible teacher Fuchsia Picket—whom *Charisma* magazine later called "a spiritual mother in the charismatic movement"[14]—wrote about the "Jezebel spirit" in her book *The Next Move of God: A Divine Revelation of the Coming Revival*.

"It is not difficult to trace the working of this Jezebel spirit in today's culture," she argued. "It energizes the feminists, and is the motivator of abortion. It is especially rampant in the entertainment industry, flaunting itself in its glamor and brazen desire to seduce the minds and affections of a nation."[15]

Also in 1994, charismatic megachurch pastor Dick Bernal, who started backing Trump in 2015, wrote about the "Jezebel spirit" in his book *When Lucifer and Jezebel Join Your Church*. While many writers in this era emphasized that the "Jezebel spirit" can be found in men and women, Bernal argued, "The Jezebel spirit primarily works through women or effeminate men."[16] Similarly, charismatic preacher Rick Godwin wrote about the "Jezebel spirit" in his 1997 book *Exposing Witchcraft in the Church*. He criticized this spirit for "her evil schemes and tactics" that have a "toxic" effect on a church.[17] To deal with a Jezebel spirit, he recommended confronting her directly and making sure she submits since "when a woman is submitted to her husband, Jezebel's tactics cannot affect that marriage."

Numerous other books in that era and more recently also use the phrase. The list of such works by charismatic preachers and

---

[14] "Bible Teacher Fuchsia Pickett Dies," *Charisma*, February 29, 2004, https://mycharisma.com/charisma-archive/bible-teacher-fuschia-pickett-dies.

[15] Fuchsia Pickett, *The Next Move of God: A Divine Revelation of the Coming Revival* (Lake Mary, FL: Charisma House, 1994), 35.

[16] Dick Bernal, *When Lucifer and Jezebel Join Your Church* (San Jose, CA: Jubilee Christian Center, 1994), 15.

[17] Rick Godwin, *Exposing Witchcraft in the Church* (Lake Mary, FL: Charisma House, 1997), 27.

"prophets" includes *Unmasking the Jezebel Spirit* by John Paul Jackson (with a foreword from Lou Engle), *Destroying the Jezebel Spirit* by Bill Vincent, *Jezebel's War with America* by Michael Brown, and *The Spiritual Warrior's Guide to Defeating Jezebel* by Jennifer LeClaire. As we've seen with other concepts pushed by leaders in the New Apostolic Reformation movement and the broader charismatic world, the theory of a "Jezebel spirit" exploded in use over the last three decades to the point that it now strikes many people as a biblical phrase. But it's not.

A phrase like "Jezebel spirit" cosplays as a biblical idea without actually being grounded in the text. This makes it malleable, as it can be used to attack people for issues well beyond those for which the two biblical Jezebels were condemned. The phrase can be applied to basically any woman one disagrees with politically, framing her as ungodly regardless of her actual religiosity or character. But with a holy veneer put on the partisan attack, it transforms political differences into a cosmic conflict of good versus evil. This rhetoric is even more alarming when Trumpian self-proclaimed "prophets" compare Trump to Jehu, the coup leader who killed the king and Jezebel so he could take the throne (as we saw in the previous chapter). The push of the "Jezebel spirit" phrase isn't just inaccurate since it's not in the Bible; it was created to weaponize scripture for political ends. That's why it matters when misogynistic partisan attacks are dressed up in religious garb—and why we must push back when Christian Nationalistic preachers try to rewrite the Bible to add new ideas.

Turn, Turn, Turn

While Christian Nationalists sometimes try to add new language and concepts to scripture, on other occasions they want to cut things out. Like Donald Trump Jr. suggested a few days before Christmas in 2021. Speaking at a conference in Arizona, he claimed that while liberals are "playing hardball," conservatives stay nice and are just "playing tee-ball"[18] (though just because Junior still needs the tee doesn't mean others haven't figured out how to throw some spin).

---

[18] Raw Story Videos, "Donald Trump Jr.: Following the Peaceful Part of the Bible Has 'Gotten Us Nothing,'" YouTube, December 19, 2021, https://www.youtube.com/watch?v=bJ7VDJdFmQU.

Thus, he urged the crowd of activists at the event sponsored by Turning Point USA, a conservative political group created by Trumpian activist Charlie Kirk, to "band together" and fight back against an alleged "cancel culture." To accomplish this, however, they'll have to put aside (ahem, cancel) some teachings of Jesus.

"We've turned the other cheek, and I understand sort of the biblical reference, I understand the mentality, but it's gotten us nothing," Trump Jr. complained. "Okay? It's gotten us nothing while we've ceded ground in every major institution in our country."

Since both Trump Jr. and Kirk attack Democrats as against churches or anti-God, the comment particularly jumped out. Trump Jr. didn't merely reject the generic idea of avoiding retaliation but specifically took issue with the substance of a biblical teaching, one offered by none other than Jesus. Yet, the attitude expressed by Trump Jr. wasn't an outlier. When Trump Sr. got a softball question from a conservative radio talk show host during the 2016 campaign to name his favorite Bible verse, the candidate proved he needed a theological tee to help him out. After hemming and hawing a bit as if he was hoping to recall a verse, he went for "an eye for an eye." However, that teaching was actually overturned by Jesus as he instead urged people to "turn the other cheek." It was almost like the elder Trump started reading the Bible from the beginning and gave up long before making it to Matthew (maybe because Trump just likes people who weren't exiled). Meanwhile, Melania Trump bragged during that campaign about her husband: "When you attack him, he will punch back 10 times harder."[19] So there goes another passage in Matthew. Forget forgiving seven times or seventy-seven times,[20] for this new gospel says hit back by a factor of ten. During the 2020 campaign, President Trump made the argument even more explicitly when asked during a Fox News town hall why he resorts to name-calling and negative attacks.

---

[19] Ali Vitali, "Melania Stumps for Donald Trump: 'He Will Punch Back 10 Times Harder,'" NBC News, April 4, 2016, https://www.nbcnews.com/politics/2016-election/melania-stumps-donald-trump-he-will-punch-back-10-times-n550641.

[20] In case Melania is reading, that's a reference to Matthew 18:21–22.

"When they hit us, we have to hit back," he insisted. "I wouldn't be sitting up here if I turned my cheek. … You can't turn your cheek."[21]

Or consider the similar rewrite offered by Dave Brat, a former U.S. congressman from Virginia who then became a senior vice president at Liberty University. As he defended Trump's tariffs in March 2025, Brat invoked the "Golden Rule," which comes a bit later in the Sermon on the Mount but is clearly in the same ethic as the cheek-turning teaching. Brat declared to a reporter: "Trump's going for reciprocity, which is basically the Golden Rule. Whatever you do to us, we're going to do to you."[22] He must be reading the Trump Bible to get that upside-down translation.

And it's not just politicians. For instance, MAGAchurch pastor Robert Jeffress of First Baptist Church in Dallas, Texas, defended his support of Trump in 2016 during an NPR interview: "I don't want some meek and mild leader or somebody who's going to turn the other cheek. I've said I want the meanest, toughest SOB I can find to protect this nation."[23] On the hypothetical ballot between Jesus and Trump, Jeffress bragged he would vote against Jesus. And he isn't the only prominent evangelical who announced himself politically as a Never Christer. There's also an absurd trend in recent years of Trumpian preachers talking about what they call "the sin of empathy." They use this language to justify their refusal to follow Jesus's teachings like the Golden Rule and love your neighbor. They think making up a new "sin" is their get-out-of-jail-free card, but this isn't a game.

Historian Kristin Kobes Du Mez documented how the militancy of White evangelicalism helped lead to Trump's rise. In her book

---

[21] Kevin Freking, "Trump Defends His Rhetoric in 1st TV Town Hall of 2020," *Associated Press*, March 5, 2020, https://apnews.com/article/virus-outbreak-donald-trump-financial-markets-ap-top-news-elections-c03cd0c-8f2a41ad0300092fff48ee4f4.

[22] Brittany Slaughter, "Economic Experts Weigh in on the Trade War Impact on the Stock Market," WSET, March 11, 2025, https://wset.com/news/local/economic-experts-weigh-in-on-the-trade-war-impact-on-the-stock-market-nancy-hubbard-david-brat-canada-march-2025.

[23] Michael Martin, "Pastor Jeffress Explains His Support for Trump," *All Things Considered*, NPR, October 16, 2016, https://www.npr.org/2016/10/16/498171498/pastor-robert-jeffress-explains-his-support-for-trump.

Jesus and John Wayne: How White Evangelicals Corrupted a Faith and Fractured a Nation, she contrasted the ethic of cheek-turning with the aggressive teachings of prominent Christian authors and speakers like Jeffress, John Eldredge, Gordon Dalbey, and Paul Coughlin. I asked her about Trump Jr.'s idea of removing the check-turning teaching from the Bible:

> Trump Jr. is perhaps a little less polished here with his "sort of" understanding of the biblical reference, but he's not exceptional in that many conservative Christian culture warriors have either ignored or explicitly rejected Jesus's command to "turn the other cheek." Conservative evangelicals, for example, for all their talk of being "Bible-believing" Christians, have been selective about which passages they view as literal and authoritative and which they readily explain away.

This matters because excising the words of Jesus—while elevating others—naturally impacts behavior. It's like how Thomas Jefferson took a literal knife to the pages of the New Testament. Reflecting his deistic notions of a God who set the world spinning and then left it alone, his personal Bible excluded miracle accounts, including those involving Jesus, that his rationalism found unbelievable. Today, Christian Nationalist politicians and preachers instead cut out the moral teachings of Jesus, which impacts how they read the Bible and act toward others. As Du Mez added:

> Among those who have embraced a militant culture-wars Christianity, these words of Christ are seen as not applicable to the current moment—whatever that moment may be—because the threats to Christianity are always perceived as so dire that a militant response is the only appropriate response for Christians, and especially for Christian men, who are seen as God-ordained protectors of faith and nation. This militancy has been cultivated in generations of Christian men who have been told by pastors and popular Christian writers that, sure, Jesus came to bring peace, but it's an

eschatological peace that comes only after his enemies are slayed. Or that you can't teach a boy to become a man by teaching him to turn the other cheek. Instead, he needs to be aggressive and to channel that aggression in a way that defends Christianity against enemies, wherever they may be found.

An edited Bible begets an edited gospel.

To cut out key passages like Matthew 5:39 will lead us on a dangerous path. Like the one at the Turning Point USA conference in Arizona. In addition to Trump Jr., another celebrated speaker was Kyle Rittenhouse, fêted as a hero after shooting and killing protesters. The organization's head, Charlie Kirk, explained why they heralded Rittenhouse.

"We brought Kyle Rittenhouse to front stage. That's a win," Kirk claimed on the Trumpian charismatic talk show *Flashpoint*. "It's a win for due process. A win for constitutional order. It's a win for presumption of innocence—all biblical values, by the way. Plenty of people were wrongfully accused all throughout the Bible, especially the Old Testament, including Jesus Christ himself."[24]

I missed the part where Jesus killed two protesters. But if you take out his words about turning the other cheek, you end up with a savior who guns people down with an AR-15—especially if they're considered those devilishly scheming liberals with a "Jezebel spirit."

Steps Toward Not Misreading the Bible Like a Christian Nationalist

1. When quoting the Bible or listening to someone who does, double-check the passage. If someone is changing what it says or adding new language, consider why and be wary of them.

---

[24] Watch the clip: Patriot Takes (@patriottakes), X, December 21, 2021, https://x.com/patriottakes/status/1473485094228840450.

2. Avoid the temptation to throw out the words of Jesus in favor of some other text. When someone does, that's a sign to reject the politics and theology they are pushing.
3. Watch out for efforts to weaponize scripture against political enemies. Much of the rewriting of the Bible is done to avoid clear teachings about loving others and doing unto others as you would want them to do unto you.

CHAPTER 9

A Non-Christian Nationalist Bible

I often call Sean Feucht the musical Forrest Gump of Christian Nationalism. He shows up with his guitar just about everywhere Christian Nationalists gather. He joined a group of Christians in the Oval Office during Donald Trump's first term to pray over the president—and he's the one in the photo reaching out over the desk to touch Trump. He performed at various iterations of the ReAwaken America Tour—including the one I attended in Branson, Missouri—along with Michael Flynn, Kash Patel, Eric Trump, Lance Wallnau, and various Trumpian "prophets." He sang at campaign events for Christian Nationalist candidates like Doug Mastriano in Pennsylvania and Kari Lake in Arizona. He's held large worship rallies on the National Mall, where he's been joined by Sen. Josh Hawley of Missouri, and led small worship sessions inside the rotunda of the U.S. Capitol and the White House in Trump's second term. And in 2023 and 2024, he launched a fifty-state tour in partnership with Charlie Kirk's Turning Point USA to hold a worship rally at every state capitol building during the run-up to the 2024 election. Billed as "Kingdom to the Capitol," he sang worship songs, pushed partisan politics, talked about Jesus, and repeated COVID-19 and election conspiracies as if he was just moving through a well-planned concert set. For one of his first stops on the tour in 2023, he showed up at the Missouri Capitol just a couple of blocks from my church and office—all while wearing a "Jesus Loves America" sweatshirt featuring a U.S. flag. On Palm Sunday.

Feucht came to assert Christian dominion over the Capitol. Denouncing a rally there on the Capitol grounds a few days earlier to support the rights of transgender people, he insisted he and his group were taking over the place and would "turn this Capitol into an altar." As a sign of that, he mentioned how he had been allowed—apparently with the help of a lawmaker—to head to a part of the Capitol off-limits from the public (yes, I'm jealous).

"I went to the very top of the Capitol rotunda. I snuck my guitar up 285 steps," he said. "I got up on the top of that rotunda and I declared, 'The kingdom of God is coming to the state of Missouri.' From this governmental principality, we say, 'The government is on your shoulders!'"

Fashioning himself like a Moses taking over the land, he insisted he had come to bring a prophetic word. With this, he employed Isaiah 9:6 to suggest the Missouri government should be ruled by Jesus (and, by extension, Feucht's crowd), thus repeating some of the errors about mistaking kingdoms that we saw in chapter 6. He also fashioned himself and the movement as modern Esthers (per an issue we considered in chapter 5) as he prayed, "We thank you, Jesus, that we get to be alive 'for such a time as this.'" Then, after featuring two ultraconservative Republican state lawmakers to offer partisan prayers, Feucht led the crowd in communion. Making this politically tinged rally the church, his team passed out the elements as part of his quest to wage spiritual battle there at the Capitol:

> Together as the church of Jesus Christ of Missouri, we're going to take communion right here. … You're going to win this war in communion because the blood of Jesus is our greatest weapon. … Let's hold up the blood. And I just declare this over the state of Missouri: The blood of Jesus is strong enough over every issue in this state, over every problem that plagues the people in this state.

People partook of the elements to show their commitment to the kingdom Feucht preached and sang about. But which kingdom was it?

When I trekked over to the Capitol for Feucht's afternoon rally, it was actually the second time I went there that day. On that Sunday morning, I had joined some other parents and Sunday School teachers as children from two downtown churches celebrated Palm Sunday by following a donkey down the street while waving palm branches and singing songs.

I loved going with my son on the "donkey parade" before he became "too old" for it. It's a vivid way of helping the kids remember the biblical story that kicks off Holy Week. And since we live in a state capital, it also subtly reminds people of the political implications of that day. We march past the Governor's Mansion, but the kids keep waving and singing no matter what Governor Pilate might think. And we march to the Capitol, not to claim it but to pass by before returning to church because we realize salvation isn't found in that temple of government. But there's also something deeply symbolic in the location of our donkey parade. The original Palm Sunday crowd was not there merely for spiritual salvation. They had political hopes. They wanted a conquering messiah to deliver them from the oppression of the Roman government. That's why the week of Passover—a holiday that commemorated God's delivering the people from the Egyptian empire—at times in the years before Jesus's entry had inspired attempted violent uprisings.

"The week often incited all-out insurrection," Jason Porterfield, author of *Fight Like Jesus*, told me as he explained that Pilate and Jesus marched in from opposite sides of the city, one with soldiers and the other on a donkey. "The week was really being set up to be a clash of two competing approaches to peacemaking. And the irony is the crowds thought Jesus was coming to bring peace using the same methods as Pilate; they just hoped he was stronger."

Many today also hope for a political strongman. But that's not the moral of Palm Sunday or the rest of Holy Week. It's not about seizing power. It's not about taking over the government.

As the kids followed the donkey near the Capitol in 2022, I noticed a crew was preparing the grounds for Feucht's rally. The stage was literally being set. A few hours later, people who supported a violent insurrection on the U.S. Capitol would sing and wave their flags on Palm Sunday (including flags common in the January 6 crowd, like the one with a pine tree that says "An Appeal to Heaven"). Not only did Turning Point USA help with Trump's rally that fateful day, but the group and Feucht continued to defend Trump and those who participated in the insurrection. And multiple times on Palm Sunday, Feucht praised the U.S. senator who most supported the effort to overturn the 2020 election and infamously gave the January 6 crowd a fist pump. That was a crowd that wanted an insurrection to remove the governmental leaders they didn't like. Much like the crowd two thousand years earlier in Jerusalem. They initially sang for Jesus, but before the week ended the people instead shouted for Barabbas the insurrectionist and proudly proclaimed, "We have no king but Caesar."[1] They didn't understand Jesus or the kingdom he brought to the capital. The wisdom of the crowds today often isn't much better.

Reading Matters

When I was a teenager, a Jehovah's Witness knocked on our door one day. Seeing her through the window and realizing why she was there, I quickly grabbed my Bible and met her at the door. As she tried to convince me, an aspiring Baptist minister, to consider her faith's teachings, she would mention a Bible verse to justify her theological talking points. Since I was the undisputed champion of my church youth group's Bible drills, I beat her each time in flipping to the passage. Noticing I had it opened, she would beckon me to read it. And that's when things fell apart for her. She apparently didn't know that the New World Translation of the Bible that Jehovah's Witnesses use makes some significant edits. For instance, John 1:1 does not say "The Word ... was God" but rather "The Word ... was a god." They literally edited the Bible to match their theology (the problem discussed in chapter 8). So when I would read a more accurate translation of the passage, she would look at her notes and back up at

---

[1] In case Sean Feucht is reading, that's John 19:15.

me with confusion. It was close, but it didn't quite support what she was supposed to say. After a few passages like this and my offering some oppositional commentary, she quickly left and went to try her luck with my neighbors.

As we watch the Christian faith remade as a nationalistic, flag-waving cry of support for powerful, imperial interests, we must recognize that addressing such theological rot and reclaiming the revolutionary faith of Jesus requires us to contend for the Bible. To confront the political threat to our democracy, we must also push back against abuses of the Bible like those explored in this book. Christians who oppose Christian Nationalism need to spend more time reading and talking about the Bible, not less. As Caleb Campbell, an evangelical pastor in Phoenix, Arizona, and author of *Disarming Leviathan: Loving Your Christian Nationalist Neighbor*, put it: "The way out of this is to out-Bible the Christian Nationalists."[2] That's basically the whole premise of this book.

Of course, it's not just reading the Bible that matters, but how. I've tried to give some suggestions throughout this book as I outlined seven noteworthy categories of heretical interpretation that view scripture as a prop, numerology, selectively literal, triumphal, pro-America, warfare, or rewritable. But four bigger admonitions are also worth highlighting, especially when it comes to specifically countering the false gospel of Christian Nationalism.

First, we must read the Bible in context. Often, Christian Nationalists pluck a verse or phrase or even just a number from the text to create new meanings around it. The Bible, however, was written by various individuals to various peoples at various points in time, all much different than our own. That's why Old Testament scholar Pete Enns of *The Bible for Normal People* podcast likes to say that we need to read the Bible with "ancient eyes." Our modern eyes, worldviews, and understandings of science, technology, and more get in our way of understanding the text. He explained:

---

[2] Caleb Campbell, "Engaging Christian Nationalists as a Mission Field," lecture at the University of Notre Dame's 2025 Catholic Social Tradition Conference, March 21, 2025.

> Reading the Bible with ancient eyes is a privilege, a challenge, and a sign of humility. And one does not have to be well-versed in ancient history to do this. Any decent study Bible, with notes, maps, and essays, is more than enough. ... Beyond that, there are mountains of popular books and commentaries that are easily accessible. It may take time to find ones that are most useful, but there should be no hurry here. This is a lifetime path.[3]

Approaching the Bible with humility would go a long way in shielding us from Christian Nationalist perspectives. Admitting that we don't understand the text or that we don't like ones we do understand is part of taking the text seriously. My goal with this book isn't for us to go tit-for-tat in an argument. Pulling a verse out of context to "beat" the Christian Nationalists is to make a mistake similar to how they regularly treat the Bible. A humble approach to scripture also means reading the Bible in community, not just in terms of a local community but also in light of centuries of Christian witness. We should be suspicious of anyone who suddenly discovers a new biblical reading. I'm pretty skeptical of a theology that's younger than a couple of shirts in my closet, like the idea of "seven mountains" we're supposed to take dominion over (seriously, I have shirts from high school older than that teaching). This doesn't mean all who went before us were always right. We're all fallible humans. But we should be suspicious of anyone suddenly finding a new revelation that no one noticed over thousands of years of careful study.

Second, we must read the Bible more from the margins by considering perspectives of theologians and pastors from other backgrounds and countries—especially those who aren't White, cisgendered, heterosexual men (though it's okay to still read such individuals, which is a good time to note I have other books you can buy). Those of us in the U.S. also need to consider ways of reading the Bible that are less Western, individualistic, and capitalistic. As New Testament scholar Angela Parker explained in her book *If God*

---

[3] Doug Stuart, "Pete Enns Tells Me So," Libertarian Christian Institute, November 28, 2014, https://libertarianchristians.com/2014/11/28/peter-enns-tells-me-so.

Still Breathes, Why Can't I?: Black Lives Matter and Biblical Authority, much of what is simply called "biblical interpretation" is only from the perspective of White male scholars, which can squash other perspectives that help us notice and understand details of a text and how to apply them today. Considering more perspectives expands our understanding. As Parker explained:

> Inspiration comes from embracing the various identities within both the biblical text and the world around us in order to fight with and for one another for justice in a world that seems to be going horribly wrong. ... As a Womanist biblical scholar, my call is to perform biblical interpretation not like a White male biblical scholar but, rather, in a way that provides flashes of table turning and table expansion. I seek to be a vessel and tool of inspiration for more people to read biblical texts more freely. I hope for an open table that is not owned by anyone and that has space for all.[4]

Additionally, since Christian Nationalism at its core centers America in God's story, listening to and centering international voices is absolutely essential. As I talk with pastors about countering Christian Nationalism, I always encourage them to focus on the global Church. Preaching about a global faith is perhaps the best way to undermine the theological foundation of Christian Nationalism. And anytime something is happening in the world, it can be helpful to remember that some Christians are likely there and impacted, which calls to mind Paul's admonition about how the whole body is to suffer when one part suffers.

Third, since Christian Nationalism in the U.S. is at its heart a glorification of the global empire, we should lift up readings of scripture that challenge the empire. Matthew Taylor, a scholar with the Institute for Islamic-Christian-Jewish Studies and author of *The Violent Take It by Force: The Christian Movement That Is Threatening Our Democracy*, argued that we need to offer a counter-witness to

---

[4] Angela N. Parker, *If God Still Breathes, Why Can't I?: Black Lives Matter and Biblical Authority* (Grand Rapids, MI: Wm. B. Eerdmans Publishing Co., 2021), 113.

Christian Nationalism by highlighting the anti-imperial parts of the Bible so that people in the pews are ready with some Bible references when confronted with the ways MAGA evangelicals and charismatics use Bible verses. As he explained:

> The early church was deeply anti-imperial and anti-authoritarian. They weren't perfect. They didn't always agree on everything. But where they were solid was that they resisted the imperial cult that demanded that they bowed to Caesar. That was why they were persecuted. We have a new imperial cult in America that's rapidly taking over. So we need to go and do New Testament Bible study.[5]

Taylor especially pointed to the Gospel of Mark as a starting place. Regardless of where you begin, I offer a hearty "amen" to his call for anti-imperial Bible studies.

Fourth, perhaps most fundamentally, an important factor when we approach the Bible is what our guiding view is. Do we read the Bible through the words and witness of Jesus, or do we instead lift up other passages over that of the one who is actually the Word? God is love, and Jesus taught us that the greatest commandments are to love God and to love our neighbors as ourselves. Those truths should color how we read the Bible overall. Historian Jemar Tisby, author of *The Color of Compromise: The Truth about the American Church's Complicity in Racism*, has argued that a difference between "the Christianity of Christ" and "White Christian Nationalism" is that the former "reads the Bible through the lens of the life and teachings of Jesus Christ" while the latter "selectively uses scripture to promote nationalist and racial ideologies."[6] With his framing, Tisby deliberately echoed the assessment of abolitionist Frederick Douglass who, after he escaped from slavery, condemned the faith of his former enslavers. However, Douglass added:

---

[5] Brian Kaylor, "Notre Dame Conference Addresses 'Pressing Crisis' of Christian Nationalism," *A Public Witness*, March 25, 2025, https://publicwitness.wordandway.org/p/notre-dame-conference-addresses-pressing.

[6] Jemar Tisby, "Recognize the difference. What other differences would you add?" Facebook, January 26, 2025, https://www.facebook.com/photo?fbid=1062938235636150&set=pcb.1062938258969481.

> What I have said respecting and against religion, I mean strictly to apply to the *slaveholding religion* of this land, and with no possible reference to Christianity proper; for, between the Christianity of this land, and the Christianity of Christ, I recognize the widest possible difference—so wide, that to receive the one as good, pure, and holy, is of necessity to reject the other as bad, corrupt, and wicked. To be the friend of the one, is of necessity to be the enemy of the other. I love the pure, peaceable, and impartial Christianity of Christ: I therefore hate the corrupt, slaveholding, women-whipping, cradle-plundering, partial and hypocritical Christianity of this land. Indeed, I can see no reason, but the most deceitful one, for calling the religion of this land Christianity.[7]

It's a harsh word, but one that's appropriate for any professed version of Christianity that seeks to replace Jesus's rhetoric about loving our neighbors and turning the other cheek with justifications for racial discrimination and calls for violently seizing power.

Lost Sheep

The goal here isn't to win a bunch of Bible arguments. It's ultimately about helping people see, hear, and know Jesus. Christian Nationalism is getting in the way. The problem we face that Peter, Paul, (and Mary,) and other early Church leaders didn't have to overcome is that the false religion of the empire uses the same name as the one we proclaim. So a lot of people think they're Christian but have been discipled not in the way of Jesus but in Christian Nationalism. They need us to help them rediscover the Bible and read it in fresh ways.

Consider a moment during a CNN report at a 2021 Trump rally in Alabama. As a reporter interviewed a Trump supporter, she explained that she got her news from "prophets of God and Newsmax and maybe

---

[7] Frederick Douglass, *Narrative of the Life of Frederick Douglass, an American Slave, Written by Himself* (New Haven: Yale University Press, 2001), 85.

a little Fox"[8] (by which I presume she meant the TV channel and not actually a little fox, since that would beg the question of what does the fox say). An anti-vaxxer at a point when the COVID-19 pandemic continued to spread despite the rollout of the vaccines, the woman explained to CNN that her opposition was because she was listening to God: "I think it is a time where God is separating the sheeps [sic] from the goats." That allusion is, of course, to a famous parable of Jesus in which the sheep are the righteous who helped "the least of these," while the goats are selfish and are cast away in judgment. The CNN reporter asked the woman what should've been an easy follow-up: Which one is she? The woman responded, "I am a goat, cause I ain't a sheep. I'm not doing what they tell me to do. I'm fighting against it." At first, I laughed at the absurdity of the woman literally flipping the parable of Jesus on its head to make the sheep the bad ones. But I got a little, well, sheepish about my attitude as I heard the words of Matthew's Gospel remind me how to be Christlike: "When he saw the crowds, he had compassion for them, because they were harassed and helpless, like sheep without a shepherd."[9]

The woman has a high view of the Bible's authority but low biblical literacy. And that's dangerous for herself and the rest of us. She hasn't been discipled well—not just in terms of reading the Bible but also in how to apply it through a lens of loving one's neighbor. Churches, pastors, and other Christians have failed this woman. Instead, she found community and meaning on Internet conspiracy sites and from false prophets and grifters. We could rightly call this woman's politics Christian Nationalism. Yet, the problem isn't that she's been too influenced by the Bible but that she hasn't read it enough. And she's not an isolated case. Such a pandemic has ripped through our churches and society for years. If we fail to confront the abuses of scripture, we leave that woman in Alabama and millions more like her to be devoured by wolves in sheep's clothing (or perhaps even in goat's clothing). That's why I try to have grace for those who have

---

[8] CNN, "'God Is Separating the Sheep from the Goats': Trump Supporter on Why She Remains Unvaccinated," YouTube, August 23, 2021, https://www.youtube.com/watch?v=Vr3ZNvv0aco.

[9] In case the CNN woman is reading, that's Matthew 9:36.

been misled even as I critique the false prophets. And it's why we must seek to reclaim the Bible from Christian Nationalists. Because this isn't ultimately about saving the Bible but helping those who have been led astray by preachers and politicians who exploit scripture and people for political power.

Acknowledgements

This is my third project with Chalice Press, following *Unsettling Lent* and *Baptizing America*. That should signal my appreciation for Brad Lyons and the whole team at Chalice. They've been excellent to work with and willing to take risks by publishing my words. I'm thankful for all the readers who support Chalice's ministry, especially those who've purchased *Unsettling Lent* and *Baptizing America*. It's been encouraging and exciting to see churches and denominational bodies in multiple mainline denominations embrace *Baptizing America* with book studies and inviting me and/or that book's coauthor (Beau Underwood) to speak about Christian Nationalism. Without such support, this new book wouldn't have come about. I look forward to many more conversations and events now as we work together to address the dangers of Christian Nationalism.

I'm thankful for the board, readers, donors, and everyone else who supports *Word&Way*. It's an honor to lead this journalism ministry that's been "contending for the word and showing the way" since 1896. I love my job, and so I'm grateful for everyone who makes it possible. In particular, I'm appreciative of the encouragement, suggestions, and inspiration from my colleagues Beau Underwood and Jeremy Fuzy. Both helped me develop various ideas that led to this book and offered support and feedback. Fortunately, Chalice brought Jeremy onto this project to serve as an editor. It's always great to work with him and I'm glad he was around to help make this book even better. I am also thankful for Rebecca Martin adeptly proofing the book, and for Kesley Houston designing the beautiful cover. It is also encouraging and humbling to receive kind words about my work from the likes of Caleb Campbell, Angela Denker, Obery Hendricks, and Drew Strait.

Finally, I'm also thankful for the support of Jen, who encourages me even when she's not interested in a topic I'm writing about at that moment. She and our son, Kagan, keep me grounded and hopeful even as I venture into odd and dark places for writing topics. And I'm grateful for my parents, former Sunday School teachers, college professors, pastors, and others over the years who taught me the Bible and kindled a passion for reading and studying it more. But don't hold any of them responsible for something you didn't like in the book—I want all the criticism (I'm an Enneagram 8, so bring it on).

About the Author

Brian Kaylor is a Baptist minister with a Ph.D. in political communication. A former professor of political communication and advocacy studies, he has led *Word&Way* as president and editor-in-chief since 2016. He previously served at churches and denominational organizations affiliated with the Cooperative Baptist Fellowship, American Baptist Churches USA, and Southern Baptist Convention.

Kaylor is the author or coauthor of multiple books, including *Baptizing America: How Mainline Protestants Helped Build Christian Nationalism* and *Unsettling Lent: A Devotional*. *Baptizing America* won top book awards in 2025 from both the Associated Church Press and the Religion Communicators Council.

Kaylor writes regularly about faith and politics at *A Public Witness*, an award-winning e-newsletter from *Word&Way*. Learn more and subscribe at publicwitness.wordandway.org. Kaylor's writings have been published by numerous outlets, including *Boston Globe*, CNN, *Houston Chronicle*, *Kansas City Star*, *Nashville Tennessean*, *Sojourners*, and *Washington Post*.

Kaylor serves as vice chair on the board of trustees for Americans United for Separation of Church and State. He has also served on the board of the Baptist Peace Fellowship of North America and as chair of the resolutions committee for the Baptist World Alliance.

Connect with Kaylor online to keep tracking how Christian Nationalists misuse the Bible

- Sign up for the e-newsletter *A Public Witness*: publicwitness.wordandway.org
- Follow Kaylor on YouTube and Bluesky: @BrianKaylor

Scripture Index

Genesis 2:1 — 30
Genesis 12:3 — 44-48
Genesis 31 — 18
Genesis 45:1 — 33
Genesis 50:20 — 68-69
Exodus 20 — 16, 19-24, 31
Leviticus 11:10-12 — 42-43
Joshua 1:9 — 80
Joshua 6 — 99-100
Judges 7:1 — 4
1 Samuel 15 — 76-77
1 Samuel 17 — 100
2 Kings 9-10 — 59, 87-91, 100, 107
2 Kings 13 — 37
2 Chronicles 7:14 — 78-80, 96, 100
Esther 4:14 — 2, 58-65, 100-101
Nehemiah 6 — 30
Psalm 7:1 — 4, 29
Psalm 23:4 — 50
Psalm 33:12 — 73, 80
Psalms 42-43 — 31
Proverbs 10:1 — 52
Proverbs 14:34 — 73
Provers 22:15 — 48-53
Proverbs 23:13-14 — 48-53
Proverbs 26:4 — 50
Proverbs 29:17 — 48-53
Ecclesiastes 4:12 — 38
Song of Songs 4:8 — 47
Isaiah 9 — 47, 118
Isaiah 19 — 46, 48
Isaiah 23:11-12 — 46
Isaiah 44:1 — 34
Isaiah 45:1 — 33-34

Isaiah 47: 1 — 34
Isaiah 54:17 — 100
Ezekiel 21:1-3 — 47
Ezekiel 30:5 — 47
Daniel 8:21-22 — 46
Amos 2 — 47-48
Amos 6:11 — 28
Habakuk 3:9 — 36
Malachi 4 — 30
Matthew 5:13-14 — 73-77, 85, 100
Matthew 5:38-39 — 95, 111-114
Matthew 7:12 — 112
Matthew 9:36 — 126
Matthew 10:34 — 101
Matthew 16:18 — 84-85
Matthew 18:21-22 — 111
Matthew 25:31-46 — 126
Matthew 26:52 — 101
Luke 10:25 — 31
John 1:1 — 120
John 11:35 — 81
John 18:33-40 — 85
John 19:15 — 120
Romans 3:23 — 104
1 Corinthians 9:12 — 31
2 Corinthians 3:17 — 55-57
2 Corinthians 10:4 — 18, 92-93
Ephesians 4:3 — 97
Ephesians 6:11 — 25-28, 61, 92-97, 100-101, 103-105
Colossians 3-4 — 30
2 Timothy 1:7 — 80-81
Hebrews 4-5: 30
Revelation 2:20 — 107-108
Revelation 3:16 — 12

Topical Index

Ahn, Ché 58, 88, 91, 99
Baptist 1, 6, 9, 45, 49-50, 57, 67, 77, 80, 82-83, 93, 98, 108, 112, 120, 131
Barbie 18-19
Biden, Joe 2, 34-36, 67-68, 93, 103
Boebert, Lauren 32, 94-95
Brueggemann, Walter 11-12
Cahn, Jonathan 58, 88-91, 99
Campbell, Caleb 121, 129
Catholic 8, 22, 29, 31, 74, 99, 121
Chancey, Mark 21-22
Chick-fil-A 16-17, 83
Clinton, Hillary 25, 34
COVID 126
Cyrus 32-35, 87
Dallas, Kelsey 74, 101
David 4, 55, 57-58, 64, 66, 87, 100
DeSantis, Ron 103-105
De La Torre, Miguel 67
Denker, Angela 85, 129
Donnelly, Jenny 58-59, 88
Douglass, Stephen 124-125
Du Mez, Kristin 112-114
Egypt 5, 21, 46-48, 68, 119
Engle, Lou 58, 88, 110
Enns, Pete 121-122
Episcopal 13-14, 71-72
Esther 2-3, 58-65, 88, 118
Evans, Rachel Held 43
Falwell Jr., Jerry 55-57, 64
Feucht, Sean 117-120
Flynn, Michael 66, 74, 88, 92, 99, 117

Fuzy, Jeremy 23, 25, 129
Gagné, André 8, 32
Gaza 44-46, 48
Greene, Marjorie Taylor 32, 69
Harris, Kamala 58-59, 88, 106, 108
Homosexuality 36, 42-43, 54
Heston, Charlton 20, 22
Israel 34, 44-48, 73, 76, 83, 91, 99, 107
January 6, 2021 7-8, 68, 88, 92-93, 99, 100, 102, 120
Jenkins, Jack 13
Jefferson, Thomas 11, 113
Jeffress, Robert 14, 45, 48, 112-113
Jehu 80, 87-91, 98, 100, 107
Jezebel 59, 87-91, 100, 105-110
Johnson, Mike 44, 48, 67-68, 95
Joseph 5, 33, 68-69
Joshua 1
Kansas City Chief 36-38
King James Version 1, 17-19, 21
King Jr., Martin Luther 55
Kirk, Charlie 25-26, 32, 69, 103, 111, 114, 117
Kruse, Kevin 20
Lake, Kari 95-96, 117
Lakoff, George 98
Lane, David 82-85
Laurie, Greg 63
Liberty University 55-57, 112
Lindell, Mike 35, 92, 99
Lobster 41-42
Locke, Greg 18-19, 92, 99
Mastriano, Doug 32, 117

135

Mennonite 10, 101
Missouri 1-4, 22-23, 35, 82-84, 93, 117-120
Moore, Russell 78-79
Moses 1, 5, 15, 19-21, 24, 68, 90, 118
National Association of Christian Lawmakers 21, 68
Noem, Kristi 61, 80-81
Obama, Barack 34
Oklahoma 48-53
Onishi, Bradley 81
Parker, Angela 122-123
Patel, Kash 66, 88, 117
Pence, Mike 44-45, 60
Pew Research Center 5, 10-11
Perry, Samuel 5-6
Pilate 85, 119
PRRI 101
Robinson, Mark 83, 94
ReAwaken America Tour 18, 35-36, 60-61, 66, 74, 91-93, 117
Republican National Convention 25-28, 61, 74, 79-81, 100-101
Seidel, Andrew 93
Seven Mountain Mandate 32, 37, 58, 74, 122
Sewell, Lorenzo 27, 61
Stone, Roger 88, 92, 99
Strait, Drew 10, 101, 129
Swift, Taylor 29, 36
Taylor, Mathew 8, 90-91, 123-124
Ten Commandments 19-24, 31
Texas 16, 19-22, 63, 68, 74, 83, 112
Tisby, Jemar 124

Trump, Donald 2, 10, 13-16, 25-28, 32-35, 37, 55-61, 63-64, 66, 69, 71-72, 75, 79-80, 87-89, 96, 100, 111-112, 117
Tyler, Amanda 6-7
United Methodist 2, 21
Underwood, Beau 6, 8, 72-75, 91, 94, 104, 129
Vance, J.D. 27, 32, 71, 90
Wallnau, Lance 32-39, 58, 66, 74, 87, 99, 106, 117
White-Cain, Paula 27, 61, 64, 83
Whitehead, Andrew 5, 81-82
Winthrop, John 75-77

Looking for the bigger picture?

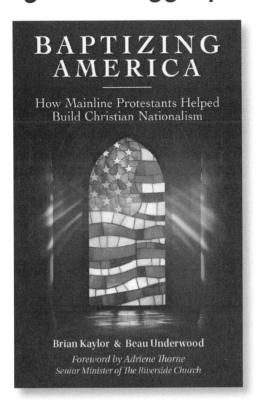

Continue the conversation with
Baptizing America: How Mainline Protestants Helped Build Christian Nationalism
by Brian Kaylor and Beau Underwood.
This groundbreaking book reveals how well-intentioned churches became entangled in the rise of Christian Nationalism—and what faithful resistance looks like today.

Available now from Chalice Press and wherever books are sold.

ChalicePress.com